In *Mother's Milk*, Rachel helped me ide⸺ed hole I felt in my heart. *I Gave Her a Name* helps me understand that there is not so much a hole in my heart, but a space taken and filled by Her. Rachel's poems are like getting whiffs of Heavenly Mother. They are comforting and encouraging. They help lead my thoughts and heart in Her direction. Growing up in a church where scripture is always words of men, I've always hoped one-day ancient scripture from women would be discovered. Rachel's poems on Heavenly Mother are modern scripture in every sense of the word. There is no more time to wait for someone else to define Her for us. Knowing Her is far too important. It is time for us to do what our sisters before us may not have been able to. I'm so grateful for Rachel's words to help light the way.

—Rosemary Card
Q.Noor CEO and author of *Model Mormon*

Rachel Hunt Steenblik and Ashley Mae Hoiland are pilgrims, dreamers, explorers in search of our Heavenly Mother and the country where she dwells. Together they have created a record of their journey, an exploration in visual and literary art, of their search. They search everywhere—looking back at mothers and grandmothers and forward to mothering their own daughters and sons. They consider giving birth, nursing, and nurturing children as experiences women share with their Mother. They examine seasons, maple trees, the moon, dragonflies, spiders, bears and eagles as metaphors for Her beauty, fierceness, and power. They re-read, re-write, and re-interpret scripture to apply to women as well as men. They consider Eve, Mary, Emmeline, Emma, Sophia, Penelope, Hannah, and many other women for clues. They learn individual lessons about Mother from a broad community of friends, family, writers, and poets (the sources are indicated in page after page of notes at the end of the collection). Hoiland's drawings, evocative in both line and color, invite a deeper and prolonged attention to Hunt Steenblik's poems. These two fine artists attempt to reach through language and visual art toward spiritual truth. That attempt requires openness, simplicity, repetition, pauses, and space for the reader. This is a book to read slowly, to consider, to savor. The gifts it offers will last.

—Susan Elizabeth Howe,
co-editor of *Discoveries: Two Centuries of Poems by Mormon Women* and author of *Salt*

What Ashmae and Rachel Taught me. You can hold truths in your heart so precious, you may not have words for them. I found so many of them in *I Gave Her a Name*. I feel closer to Heavenly Mother in a way that I have never experienced before because I wasn't looking for Her. Perhaps, she is closer than we think because we all have some of our Heavenly Mother in us. She is with us, too.

—Karim Jones
writer at dreamsinspanglish.com

Hunt Steenblik's words inspire us to find our Mother in heaven and in earth; in women's words we know and wish we knew; in mothering and longing to be mothered; in scripture and in words that should be scripture. *I Gave Her A Name* articulates the deep-seated desire more and more women and men feel to know Her and feel Her near, and in reading Hunt Steenblik's words, we draw closer to Her. This book is a gift for womankind.

—Lexie Kite, Ph.D. and Lindsay Kite, Ph.D.
Co-Directors of Beauty Redefined

The stirring words of Rachel draw you along to a new and nuanced reverence for our Mother in Heaven. Dive in and luxuriate in the richness of thought and emotion.

—McArthur Krishna
co-author of *Girls Who Choose God* and
Our Heavenly Family, Our Earthly Families

Hunt's poems, like Hoiland's images, place earth and sky and human figures in holy superposition, drawing women and mothers and children into the light of day. As all powerful art does, the collection left me wanting to sit very still for a long time and, at once, to immediately get up and do something useful.

—Adam S. Miller
author of *Letters to a Young Mormon* and *An Early Resurrection*

I Gave Her a Name is a balm, a serial prayer, a pool of riversmooth stones. Readers are invited to hold each poem and image, feel the cool heft in their palms, the weight each imparts. These inspired micropoems and drawings translate the ordinary and everyday into manifold occasions for regarding the Mother. Healing is Her(e).

—Dayna Patterson
co-editor of *Dove Song: Heavenly Mother in Mormon Poetry*

As Mother's Milk was the crescent moon of poetry exploring the feminine divine, *I Gave Her A Name* is the waxing gibbous, casting light along the path of discovery as we take courage by uttering Her name, awaiting the full illumination She has to offer. Rachel's words and AshMae's drawings remind us that, like the moon, She is always there even if we cannot see Her.

—Sara Vranes
midwife

I Gave Her
a Name

By Common Consent Press is a non-profit publisher dedicated to producing affordable, high-quality books that help define and shape the Latter-day Saint experience. BCC Press publishes books that address all aspects of Mormon life. Our mission includes finding manuscripts that will contribute to the lives of thoughtful Latter-day Saints, mentoring authors and nurturing projects to completion, and distributing important books to the Mormon audience at the lowest possible cost.

I Gave Her a Name

Written by
Rachel Hunt Steenblik

Illustrated by
Ashley Mae Hoiland

BCC
PRESS

For information contact
By Common Consent Press
4062 S. Evelyn Dr.
Salt Lake City, UT 84124-2250

Cover design: Ralph Steenblik with D. Christian Harrison
Cover illustration: Ashley Mae Hoiland
Book design: Andrew Heiss

www.bccpress.org

ISBN-10: 1-948218-12-7
ISBN-13: 978-1-948218-12-2

10 9 8 7 6 5 4 3 2 1

Rachel

For Hyrum and Joseph,
my poet brothers,
and for the baby inside of me.

Ashmae

The paintings in this book are for all the women in my life
who for too long did not have permission to name, and
for the many who are just now realizing that they do.

Acknowledgements

Rachel Hunt Steenblik   BCC Press, thank you for giving my voice a platform. Cora and Søren, thank you for teaching me what it means to be a mother seeking the Mother. You are on every page. Claudia Hunt, thank you for teaching me what it means to be a daughter seeking the Mother, and for helping me so fully to feel a mother's love. Hyrum Hunt, Joe Hunt, Cumorah McOmber, Liahona Hunt Patterson, Charity Hunt, and Sam Hunt, thank you for teaching me what it means to be a sister. Larry Hunt, thank you for supporting me in every project I've ever done, including this one. Ashmae Hoiland, thank you for saying yes to this project. Your work is exquisite. The book would not be the same without it. Annie K. Blake, thank you for your help with the book's title. William Thomas, thank you for telling me the world needed more of my work. Reija Rawle and Joe Hunt, thank you for being early readers and encouragers. Members of MoPoWrimo, thank you for your feedback on specific poems. Kristine Haglund, thank you for once again adding your gentle and wise editing. Andrew Heiss, thank you for your remarkable layout and typesetting expertise. Christian D. Harrison, thank you for your work on the cover. David Paulsen and Martin Pulido, I'm forever grateful for the opportunity to have researched Heavenly Mother with you. It changed my whole life. Spencer Steenblik, thank you for your support and co-parenting that made this book possible. Readers of *Mother's Milk* and of *I Gave Her a Name*, thank you, thank you.

Ashmae Hoiland   Like Rachel, I am grateful for the work that BCC Press has done to uplift women's voices and give us the freedom to pursue projects of the heart and mind. Thank you to Rachel, above all for believing in this work and for allowing me to be a part of it. I still remember when we talked of it many years ago and to see it come together here means a great deal. I have always been impressed with your quiet ability to say big things. Thank you to the many women and men who inspired these paintings: my children, Rachel's children, our parents and siblings, our ancestors, Alice Walker, Harriet Tubman, Hildegard of Bingen, Hilma af Klint, Mary Oliver, Maya Angelou, Claudia Rankine, Jesmyn Ward, Tracy K. Smith, Elizabeth Bishop, Janan Graham Russell, Kim Johnson, Susan Howe, Kristin Matthews, Zina Bennion, Sara Vranes, the moon, mother nature, and of course, Rachel Hunt Steenblik.

At a Pulpit

I. Boston, 2009.
I stood timid at a pulpit
and bore simple testimony
of Heavenly Mother's love
and existence for the first
time. I said it made me feel
like I had a place in heaven
and on earth. I sat down
and shook for whole minutes
afterward.

II. Brooklyn, 2013.
I wrote a single Heavenly
Mother poem while walking,
now called "Motherless Milk,"
then dreamt that night
that I stood at a pulpit
reading five. I woke to
nurse my new baby
and wrote them.

III. Jersey City, 2018.
My four-year-old daughter
stood beside me at a pulpit
where I gave a whole talk
on mother lines. I weaved
from my grandmothers, to
my mother, to myself, before
weaving to Christ who gathers
us under his wings and then to
Heavenly Mother. When I finished
speaking, my daughter climbed
on the stepstool and offered
her own mini-talk. She said,
My name is Cora. I believe
Heavenly Mother and Heavenly
Father love us. Sometimes
people are naughty to Heavenly
Mother and Heavenly Father,
but they can apologize.
She did it easily and simply.

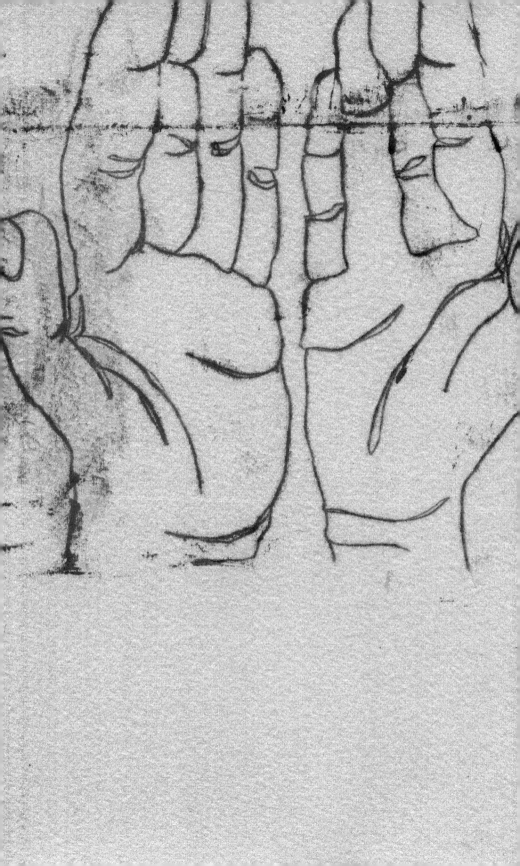

A Name
When Eve walked among
the animals and named them—
nightingale, redshouldered hawk,
fiddler crab, fallow deer—
I wonder if she ever wanted
them to speak back, looked into
their wide wonderful eyes and
whispered, *Name me, name me.*
                    —Ada Limón

Poetry Mommy
The Mother
introduces Herself,
I am the God
of rain and stories.

She writes poems
in the stars for
us to read.

Polaris
She is my
north star,
my little,
big compass
that dips
down from
the sky
and shines.

Girl Moon
C:
The Moon is following us.
The Moon is following us.

he:
It looks like She is.
It looks like She's with us
all the way.

My Daughter Talks to God

C:
*Mommy. I really,
really need help.*

She:
*I hear you, but I cannot
help you right now.*

C:
*Yes right now.
Mommy, I can't do this
by myself.*

God Talks to My Daughter

She:
*Please stop yelling at me.
I can hear you.*

C:
*I can hear you better if I yell.
I was kind of far away from you.*

What Joel Taught Me
The Mother poured out
Her spirit upon
Her children and
your daughters and sons
shall prophesy,
your old women
shall dream dreams,
your young women
shall see visions.

The Power
There are whispers
of a power, a fern-
shaped lightning
that's been there
all along,
passed from
palm to palm,
hand to hand,
young women
to old women,
that's now even
in babies.

As an Eagle

The Mother
bears us on
Her wings and
brings us
back to
Herself.

As an Eagle, II

The Mother
stirs up
Her nest and
flutters over
Her young.
She spreads abroad
Her wings and
takes them,
bears them on
Her wings.

As a Bear

The Mother meets them
as a bear, bereaved of
Her whelps, and will
rend the caul of their
heart.

The Great She Is
Is She not a woman
and a sister?
She Is.

What Sofia Taught Me
The Mother
looks beautiful,
but She is also
brave and smart.

Before
Before
She was a
mother,
She was a
lover.
Before
She loved
others,
She loved
Herself.

Ampersand
The Mother believes
in ampersands.
She is a mother,
& a lover,
& an artist,
& a poet.
She embraces
Her own and.

What Lin Taught Me
The Mother is not a maiden
in need of defending.
She is grown.

Men take Her name and
they rake it through the mud,

but Her name's
been through a lot.
She can take it.

Space
The Mother is not afraid of
Her growing body,
Her still swollen breasts,
Her soft belly.
She knows
She deserves to
take up space.

She knows
Her space
brought forth
the world.

The Graver
The Mother will not
forget me, She has
carried me within Her
belly. Her walls were
continually before me.

What Anna Taught Me

The question, *Where do
you come from?*
has a first answer
that's not a country,
or an ethnicity,
or a language
but a Mother.

Your Mother Who is In
Heaven Gives Good Gifts

When Her daughter asks,
She gives banana bread and
a pocket to hold stones
for tiny rock collections.

She Succors the Weak

She holds Her
children's hands
which hang down,
and puts Paw Patrol
band-aids on
scraped knees.

Another Good Gift

The Mother
loves to give
Her children
ice cream,
salted caramel,
pistachio, mint
chocolate chip,
raspberry sherbet,
butter cream, in
waffle or sugar
cone, two scoops
or one—
She'll let
you choose.

What Chelsea Taught Me

When your daughter asks
you to sing, *Heavenly
Mother song,*
it's ok if it throws you
for a loop
at first. At second
you can sing,
"A Child's Prayer,"
Heavenly Mother,
are you really there?

She is there.
She is listening.
We are Her children.
Her love now surrounds us.

What Wonder (Re)Taught Me

What it's like to be a child again,
nervous, before a stage,
peeking out into the audience
to try to find your Parents,
but the lights are dim
and it's hard to see. You think,
Where are my parents!?
until you see them and
feel fine.

Sometimes

Sometimes middle-aged women
transform into middle-aged
Goddess of regal beauty,
with long hair the same color
as yours, and strong, delicate
hands knitting clouds,
who say, over and over,
I hope you would listen to me,
because I love you, and,
Of course you know me!
I am your Mother.

My Daughter Talks to Our Christmas Tree

She told me, *I thought
the tree was thirsty, so
I got Her some water,*
then told the tree:
*The water's going to help.
The water's going to help.
The water's going to help.
It looks like you have a
sad memory.*

Advent

The Mother
waited, and
waited, and
waited, and
waited for
Her child—the
Light of the
whole world.

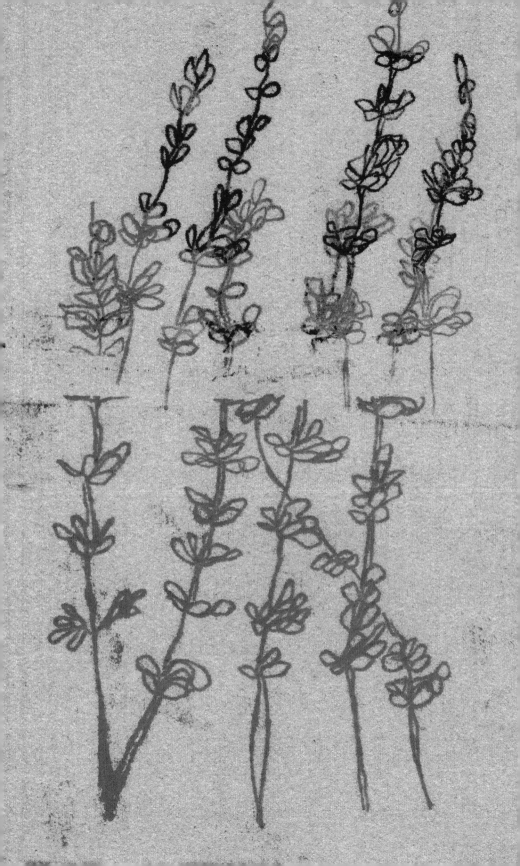

The Mother Tree
The Mother tree
grows the way She
must—branches
bent to find light.
She sheds what
must be shed
in brilliant glory,
reds, oranges, yellows.
She trusts
She can grow
new leaves,
green and soft.

The Teacher
The Mother teaches
the seasons when to
turn, with gentle
whispering,
Fall.
Fall.
Fall.

Spring.
Spring.
Spring.

Mother Time
She is before time
and after. She is
Tuesdays. And also
July. And sometimes
She's never.

To See If We've Called
The Mother is not immune
from the allure of notifications.
She checks Her phone
hundreds of times a day
to see if we've called, if we've
texted, if we've emailed.
She checks every app.

Tiptoes
Sometimes the Mother
gets homesick for us,
and tiptoes to earth
to visit us.

Where in the World is Heavenly Mother?
She is more elusive
than Carmen Sandiego.

A Mother Cries
Sometimes a God sleeps
and a mother cries
desperate for Her
in the night.

Still Life
She holds
mothers and
babies born
too soon
and still, and
weeps,
whispering
whispered names
and blessings.
She counts
their life.

What Margaret Taught Me
Our Mother sits
still with the dying
and the woman in
labor. She cries
with the outcast.

The Unseen Mother

The unseen Mother
sees mothers,
as well as all those
who are
forgotten—
refugees,
immigrants,
widows,
orphans,
strangers,
Others.
She bids us,
See them.

Proxies

Heavenly Mother would
hold our hair back if
She could, when
we throw up. Instead,
She sends proxies
having authority—
earth mothers,
fathers, midwives.
They give tiny sips of
water, fruit popsicles, and
clean us up, as many times
as needed.

Hidden Mother

Sepia prints
hint at infant
sons, daughters
held by hidden
hands, on hidden
laps, hidden mothers—
covered,
curtained,
veiled, but
there.

New

The Mother knows
about new things,
newborns, new moons,
new leaves, new years—
She cradles them gently.

Jet Lag

What it's like
to be a baby
being born,
switching from
day to
night, from
heaven to
earth.

Sand Standing
I carried Cora in
my womb, then
on my lap on a plane
between two men
four weeks later
for hours of
her hunger,
her need to sleep
but not sleep.

The next morning I held
her tight to my chest while
standing on the sand,
standing in for the Mother,
tired, still sore from torn flesh
split open, veil bloody to
bring life, this life,
this girl, too new
(born) to stand, to walk,
to smile. New to
absence, to hunger, to
fatigue,
the Pacific,
our only pacifier.

Lost Girl

The lost girl cried,
And I am your child,
before falling on her
knees and pleading,
O Heavenly lady, be
my Mother!

Matryoshka Dolls

Cora inside
Rachel inside
Claudia inside
Zena inside
Allie inside
Sarah inside
Ann inside
Maria inside
Hannah inside
…
Eve inside
Heavenly Mother.

Mother Lines

Mother lines.
We all have them,
come from them,
one maternal,
one paternal.

My own maternal:
Cora, daughter of
Rachel, daughter of
Claudia, daughter of
Zena, daughter of
Allie, daughter of
Sarah, daughter of
Maria, daughter of
Ann, daughter of
Hannah, daughter of
who? I don't know.
It's where my record
breaks.

My own paternal:
Cora, daughter of
Rachel, daughter of
Larry, son of
Billie, daughter of
Vivian, daughter of
Luisa, daughter of
Mary, daughter of
who?

Break, break,
b r e a k.

What Coco and Channing Taught Me
Our ofrendas should not be bare,
should not be missing Mother,
Father, Grandmother, Grandfather,
Great Grandmother, Great Grandfather,
who should be there.
Picture Them.

What Heidi Taught Me
Mitochondrial DNA,
Mother DNA,
mDNA,
is mother-line
passed from
a Mother to
Her children
unchanged,
generation after
generation after
generation,
giving us
the exact same mDNA
as our Mother,
and Her Mother,
and Her Mother,
and Hers.

Sacred Scraps

She learned how to quilt
from Her mother,
who learned it
from Her mother,
who learned it
from Hers,
sacred scraps
pieced together
to make whole.

A Quilt Cut With Hands

A quilt was cut with
a Woman's hands
holding brass scissors—
blue, and silver, and gold
cloth broken to pieces
together, before being
rearranged and stitched
back together again.
The new pieces became
a great quilt and filled the
whole earth.

The/Her
The rivers,
Her blood, moving;
the banks,
Her veins;
the mountains,
Her breasts;
the forests,
Her lungs–
our breath;
the earth,
Her heart
beating.

After Creation
After creation,
the Mother needed
to rest. But,
before She slept,
She held the world
to Her skin and
sighed, *You
are good.*

The Reason I Could Trust
She is why
I hoped when
I was on my
Mother's breasts,
the reason
I could trust.

Postpartum
After creation,
the Mother rested
Her sorrow, Her
emptiness and fullness,
Her softness that remained
for a long time.

Cocoon

The Mother wanted
to wrap
a cocoon
around herself
and become
a butterfly,
but She was
a dragonfly
nymph
crawling out
of calm water
onto a stem
to shed
Her skin

perching shyly
on the ledge
before knowing
She
had changed.

Chrysalis

Maybe She has
been a butterfly,
too. Maybe before
that a caterpillar
in a chrysalis,
losing every part of
Her self—Her eyes, Her
hands, Her memories,
Her heart—before
turning into
something new.

To My Mother and Also Child
I haven't heard
your heartbeat
yet,
but I feel you
sometimes
softly.

Quiet Place
If She can't speak,
can She not hear?
Is Hers a quiet
place? Does She
sign, teaching us
Her words?
Mama, Milk, Baby,
I, Love, You.

Cora Talks to God, Again and Again
C:
I was just really thirsty
for your milk.

Mother Necessity
She's the Mother of
invention, of light bulbs,
of cereal combined with
milk, of peanut butter and
jelly, of sliced bread.

The Lamplighter
The Mother says
Good morning as
She puts out Her lamp and
Good evening as
She lights Her lamp
again.

C on the Holy Spirit
She's whispering so
we need to hear it.
Don't talk a bit because
She's whispering
in your ears.

Knocks

The Mother
stands
at the
door and
knocks and
knocks
waiting for us
to answer.

As Invisible

The Mother is
as invisible as a
specter, a holy
ghost.

Lost

The Mother has
lost things
precious to
Her, too—
hair ties, pens,
chapstick, keys,
favorite hoodies,
bicycles,
homes, cities,
Her way,
memories, clarity,
lovers,
love.

Her Grief
I heard Her
wolf howl
wailing
when Her
Sister died,
a chorus
brought
to one,
the moon
Her own
witness.

What Claudia Taught Me
The Mother has a
Mother and
Sister, who—even if
lost—will always be
Hers.

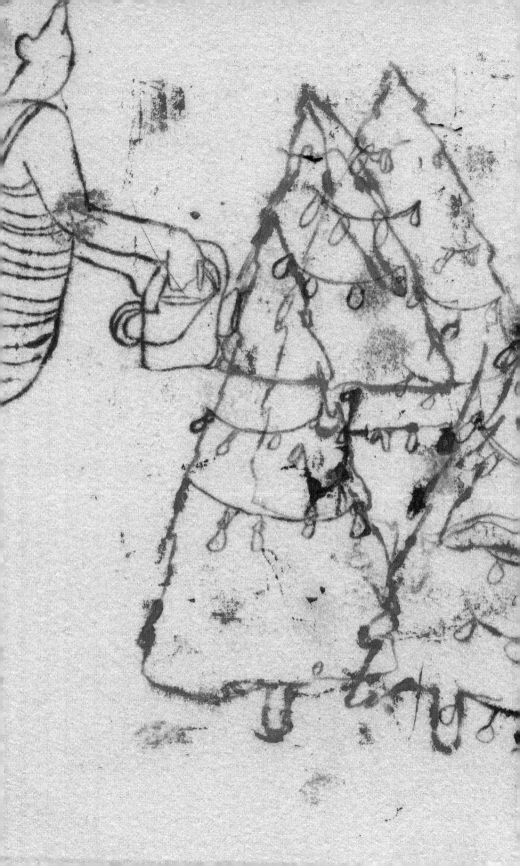

Something Soft as a Breast
One night, my daughter
already weaned two years,
told her nursing brother,
That breast is my pillow;
that breast is my milk,

writing again Carol Lynn's
poem of a Motherless house,
lying awake listening
and burying her face
in something
soft as a breast.

We are all children,
crying for our Mother
in the night.

Liminal Mother
She is the place
between waking
and sleeping.
She is waking
slowly.

Whole Hearted
Søren didn't root
for his Mother's breast,
head nuzzling from side to side,
mouth open, ready to suckle.
He threw his whole body,
limbs thrashing in urgent,
ungentle rooting

Her Breasts
Her breasts
cracked and bled
for us.

Home
When the Mama asked Her daughter
what home meant to her
the daughter was silent.
When She asked again,
the daughter pointed at Her.
The Mama questioned,
I'm your home?
The daughter nodded,
Yes.

Where We Belong
Where do I belong? the girl asks.
Mommy, you belong with me,
the girl answers.

Somewhere to Lay His Head
When Jesus
had nowhere
to lay
His head,
His Mother
was a soft place.

On the First Day of the Year
On the first day
of the year,
look at the Moon.
Spend time trying
to see Her, behind
trees, behind bends,
behind mountains,
the super Moon in
the super sky.

What Spencer Taught Me

The Moon and
Sun(Son) are out
at the same
time. It's just
harder to
see.

And, it's always
disappointing
when you
take photos of
the Moon.

Stretched

The Mother stretched
forth Her body
almost all the
day long.

The Sun

The Sun(Son) is a
reflection of Her
light, Her
warmth.

Her Brightness and Glory
Her brightness and glory
wants to be described
even though it's hard.
She is total brightness,
then darkness,
then brightness again.

Their Sum
The Mother Moon and
Sun(Son) combined
cannot be looked at—
Their sum, totaled
too powerful
for our eyes.

They gift gentle
shadows, easy
on our eyes,
thousands of tiny
crescent moons
refracted
through the
trees.

Memory Capsules

We carry Her words
whispered, tiny
cracks of light
that break through,
memory droplets—
capsules from heaven
stronger than
the veil.

We Too

The Mother sighs
into the wind
Me too.
The earth picks up
Her breath,
Me too
We too.
They weep,
for their daughters
and
Themselves.

Well Behaved Women
The Mother loves women,
both behaved and
not behaved.
She knows
their stories,
herstories,
deserve to
be told.

Like Emmeline
She believes in women,
especially thinking women.

Relief
She and Emma
did something
extraordinary.
They expected
extraordinary
occasions and
pressing calls.

What Karim Taught Me
The Mother would cross any border,
She would climb any wall,
She would do anything for Her children.

She Witnesses
She hears mothers
and babies separated,
separately crying
in the night.
She witnesses their
heart cracked
trauma tears,
sends angels to
sit with them
and humans to
fight for them.

With Eyes Closed
With eyes closed,
She knows the sound
of the soft pads of
Her children's feet
touching earth.

Are You My Mother
When the baby bird came home,
the Mother came, too.
Do you know who I am? She asked.
Yes, the baby bird answered.
You are a bird,
and you are my Mother.

Stoic Mother
Is She a stoic?
Does She grit Her teeth
and scoop Her children up
when they fall down,
crashing on scooters and
marriages? Or does
She scream, *Damn it*,
from fear and trembling
knowledge that despite
Her efforts they will
get hurt?

Helicopter Parent

Heavenly Mother is not a helicopter parent.
She lets us make our own mistakes.

Attachment Parent

Heavenly Mother is not an attachment parent.
She might have been, in the world of spirits,
but She isn't now.

French Parent

Heavenly Mother may be a French parent.
She is a believer in *the pause*,
fruits and vegetables, and doing our nights.

Free-range Parent

Heavenly Mother is a free-range parent.
She let Eve eat the fruit from every tree.

Sophia

She is Metis,
the mother of
Wisdom, and
Athena and
Minerva, Her
daughters.
She is Proverb's
Wisdom. She is
Sophia.

Borders

She borders on
wild and tame,
mercy and
justice, joy and
sorrow, goodness
and something less
than goodness,
life and the absence
of life, and wisdom and
the choice before the
fruit was eaten.

Through
The Mother passed
through sorrow
as easily as we pass
through rain, through
woods, through
oceans, through
doorways, through
classes, through
birth, through
death, through
sadness, through
joy, through
good, through
evil, to gain
knowledge.

Her Hunger
The Mother still
gets hungry
for pomegranates;
grapes; white fruits;
pickles; cheese;
bread made with
whole wheat, olive
oil, and honey;
cotton candy.

What Fiona Taught Me

Philo of Alexandria
said Sofia—
Wisdom—
was the
wife of God,

and in the no longer-
extant Gospel
of the Hebrews,
Jesus said,
My mother, the
Holy Spirit took
me just now by
one of my hairs
and carried me off
to Mt. Tabor.

The Pearl
A tale older than
Odysseus but like
an Odyssey, painting
the Mother as prudent
Penelope who stays
guarding the hearth
and waits and waits
for the Man to arrive.
It's true, and also it isn't.
The Mother waits
for all of Her children—
male and female—
and while She does
enjoy a warm fire, good
book, and a cup of tea,
She also enjoys
adventure.

She Does Not Always Guard the Hearth
The Mother gathers
sticks together—wood
for the hearth,
light to warm us.

Psalm
The Woman welcomes
the Man's laugh and the
soft scent
of His body
pressed upon
Hers.

The Song
She knew Him,
as She
was known.
She came to Him,
as He came in
to Her.
She lay with Him,
as He lay
with Her.
She acted
as She was acted
upon.

Lost and Found

The Mother found
what was lost—
hair ties, pens,
chapstick, keys,
favorite hoodies,
bicycles,
homes, cities,
Her way,
memories, clarity,
lovers,
love.

What Megan Taught Me

A pastor from New Zealand
traveled across ocean
to speak for the Mother
and to the Mother,
to minister to me.
She said the Mother
wrote on her,
mapped her pain
and joy.

What Else Megan Taught Me

You are beloved by God,
and you are loved by Her,
and you are loved by Her,
and you are loved by Her,
and you.

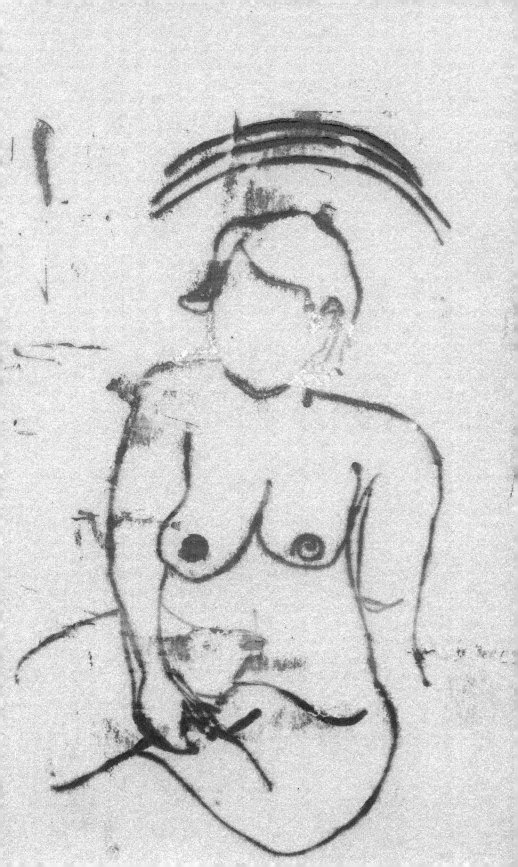

Lost You
Elizabeth watches the
Mother watching
a little boy yelling
Where did you go?
Lost you.

She watches the moon
always present,
knows *the Mother*
has never left us.

They Arise
The Mother is
a bird, like Her
Sun. They
arise from the
East with healing
in Their wings.

Of a Good Courage
The Mother asks
us to be like Herself,
strong and brave.
It's ok. We don't
need to be afraid.
She'll go with us.

What She Has Given
Before we went away,
She gave us presents
wrapped in brown
paper and tied
with gray and
white twine—
power, love, and a
sound mind.
She said,
Open.

A Trail of Small Items
The Mother is leaving
a trail of small
items,
something other than
bread crumbs,
something the birds
won't eat.
She is leaving birds.
She is leaving forests.
She is leaving mountains,
and laughter,
and heartbreak,
and the longing
for home—
to find our way back
to Her,
to at least try.

God Girl
Thea is a god girl
who knows god girl
words, like
flower-forest.

Baby's Breath
If baby's breath is
delicate white flowers
fluttering in a bunch,
Mama's breath is,
tulips, peonies,
ranunculus,
sycamore,
elm, pine,
mountains.

Tree Huggers
The Mother of
forests sacred
and not sacred
hugs the tree
huggers back.

On the 4th of July
I stood sandy
watching the
point where
Mother ocean,
Mother Atlantic,
met Her horizon,
waiting to see
the colors
match.

A Small Stream
I am a small stream,
leading into the river,
leading into Her ocean,
leading into Her love.
She welcomes me.

What Hannah Taught Me
There is nothing stronger
than a broken Woman
who has rebuilt Herself.
There is nothing stronger
than a broken Woman
who helps rebuild others.

She'll Say

When you're sexually assaulted,
come to our Mother.
She'll say,
I believe you.
She'll say,
I love you.
She'll say,
Let me sit with you.
She'll say,
Let's report this.
She'll say,
You're whole.
She'll say,
Me too.

All Day Long

All day long
She whispers,
Those that be
with you
are more.

What Steve Taught Me

No one can
be born again
without a Mother.

What Rilke Taught Me
The Mother had only
streams of milk
or tears to offer.

Words
Cora's word for
comfort was *Mama*
Søren's word for
hunger was *Mama*.

Baby Dragon
He, a baby dragon
taken from treasure—
goblets full of
precious liquid
(milk and honey);
he, nostrils flaring,
huffing warm
breath upon
my cheek.

A Prayer for Today

Mother, Father,
help me say,
*I love you, but
I cannot give you
mama's milk
anymore,* and
hold firm.

A Prayer for Tomorrow, or
The Other Side of Weaning

Mother, Father,
help me get to
the other side
of weaning,

where
we can hold
and be held
without eating.

Listening for Answers

I sat quietly across
a string, one ear
pressed into a can, as
I gazed across
at Her and
waited.

Poet Laureate

The Mother honors
the slowness of poetry,
the noticing, the sacred
pauses.

She knows it's a good way
to talk about hard things,
to make absence present.

What Steven Taught Me

The Mother is
a shepherdess
of rats and
humans.
She answers from
the sky,
She *knows*
what love is.
It even matters
to Her.
She knows
we're *all broken,*
but not unhealed.
She *can't take us*
with Her
yet,
but She *can leave us*
with a *blessing,*
can sit in rooms
with women weeping
remembering,
can offer healing milk
from Her own hands.

My Own Mother

I saw Her in
my own mother
when she, barefoot,
put on her coat
to walk outside
to say goodbye
to her daughter,
me, before I
moved across
the world
to China, unsure
when we'd see each other
again.
Heavy tears
fell down
Her face.

The Archivist

The Mother is an archivist
of Her own life,
She makes records
of places
She's cried, laughed,
studied, kissed,
walked, wrote;
benches
She sat on;
grocery stores where
ex-lovers told Her
they wanted to marry
Her and didn't.

What Joanna Taught Me
The Mother archives
every scrap of story
and every line of prose, or
poem, or personal essay,
or letter, or journal
buried under beds
or tucked away in
garages by women
who could not access
academies with gilded
towers and temperature
controlled air.
She gathers them in
one volume, for us
to hold.

Letter for a Daughter on Her Twelfth (or Possibly Eleventh) Birthday

I can't lay my hands
on your head and
give you the priesthood,
give you permission
to pass boy-blessed
bread and water from
row to row while walking
(though I would if I could).
I can tell you the little
I know of the priesstesshood
and give you books filled
with women's words, and
voices, and drawings.
I can give you knowledge
that Mormon women once
laid their hands on heads
with oil and faith
to bless and heal, and
prepare for childbirth
and that some still do.
I can give you words of
blessing in that same
spirit. Daughter, I bless you
to remember there is a
God in heaven with Her
own book of women's
words, and voices,
and drawings, and that
you may know She's
very proud of you, because
She is.

When She's Handed the Book

I.

When she's handed the book,
she clutches it to her heart
and cries,
knowing deep in her
bones that the plates
buried deep in the
earth were passed from
fathers, to sons, to
brothers, to nephews, to
grandsons—never
mothers, to daughters, to
sisters, to nieces, to
granddaughters.

When she finishes the book,
she writes of women's
hands on women's heads,
blessings before birth,
quilts that can catch you—
the deep part
of her heart
and cries.

Her fleshy tablet is tattooed with a fine scrawl
of unrepeating names for God:
Mommy, Daddy, Parents.
Her body is the veil, split open.
Her eyes are clear.

All day long she sacrifices these words
for those unburied on the earth,
mothers, daughters,
sisters, nieces,
granddaughters,
fathers, sons,
brothers, nephews,
grandsons.

She opens herself to the world
and clasps her children's bare hands.

II.
When she holds the book,
she hears voices
crying from the
dust—
prophetesses,
priestesses,
poetesses,
whispering,
Write me, write me.

III.
When she's handed the book,
she falls to the earth
and thanks God. Her
prayers have been
answered, her
cries heard.

IV.
When she's handed the book,
she walks slowly
up the mountain
and listens.

V.
When she's handed the book,
she rests her fingers on the marks—
letters pressed
upon plates.
They are cool to
her touch.

VI.
When she's handed the book,
she hands it back.
She carries libraries of
women's words deep
in her bones.
She needs new plates to
write them down.

VII.
She is handed the book.

She Carries the Book

Cora carries the book
with the story of her
birth and the
names of her
spiritual foremothers:
Claudia, Carol Lynn,
Judy, Linda,
Laurel, Susan,
Margaret, Janice,
Joanna, Lorie,
Chieko, Kate,
Janan, Gina,
Hannah, Heavenly
Mother, and me.

Big Home

I am Her little home
and She is my big.

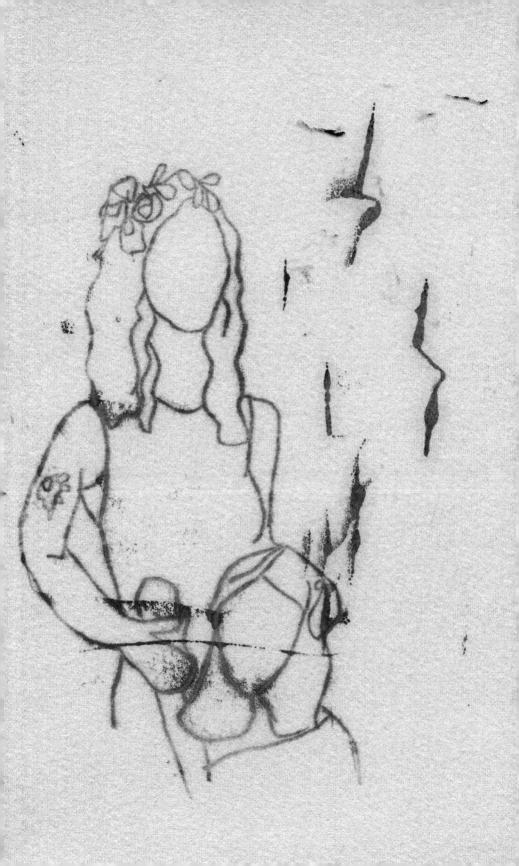

Her Birth
C asked me about
poems within
poems, like
dreams within
dreams, like
plays within
plays, like
her within
me before
her birth—
her birth
a poem,
a dream,
a play.

**What Cora Taught Me, or
The Sun and Her Little Blooms**
We are little blooms,
in need of strength
from our Mother sun
and Father rain.
They'll make us strong again.
We are little.
Our name is Little Bloom.
We're not strong.
We're not big.
Our name is supposed to be
Little Strong Blooms.

Her Name
The Mother's name
is long, in part because
our names are part of it,
woven in with everything
She loved and everything
She made. It starts, *Daffodil
Flower Unicorn* and goes on
and on.

Things that Still Delight Her
Things that still
delight Her
no matter
how many times
She sees them,
experiences them,
no matter that
She made them:
deer running,
or dancing,
or standing
still,
leaves crunching
under human
feet.

The Mother Still Delights

She saw so many
delightful things
today on one small
corner of Her world
She couldn't help
but look down and
grin—eleven leaves
letting go of their
branches, meeting
open air, meeting
earth; more than
eleven deer letting go
of earth, meeting
open air, dancing;
a small bridge over
a small river, with
a small man
fishing.

What Cora Taught Me, One Million
When the Mother spins,
She moves the world;
Her dizzy dancing
its own astronomy.

My Friend, the Moon
C asked,
Where's my friend, the Moon.
Her father answered,
He's behind the trees.

C:
You mean Her.
My mom says She's a Her.
Don't be mean to my friend.

Last Night

Last night I snuggled my children
and read them five books:
Dear Girl by Rosenthals and Hattam,
Enormous Smallness by Burgess
and Di Giacomo, *Home* by Ellis,
You Belong Here by Clark and Arsenault,
and *Love* by de la Peña and Long,
and for a time, holding books
and babies in my hands,
I felt better.

I rode a bucket bike to say
bye to the place where the
Atlantic and New Haven Sound
meet, and where I've walked
hundreds of times
with my children and myself,
including the minutes
and hours after going into labor
with my son, where
I felt the waves crash inside my body.
And last night I looked at the
veiled moon
and could almost see
Her hand.

What Rosie Taught Me

The Mother
holds us tightly,
even when we don't
want to be held,
even when we are
toddlers, backs
arched, legs kicking.
Still, She holds us.
Still, we are Hers.

What Maggie Taught Me

Mama tried,
Mama tried,
Mama tried.
(Mama tired,
Mama tired,
Mama tired.)

What Heather (Re)Taught Me

What our Mother does
is thousands of tiny,
unseen things
all day, and all day,
and all day—even
when She is tired,
especially when
She is tired.

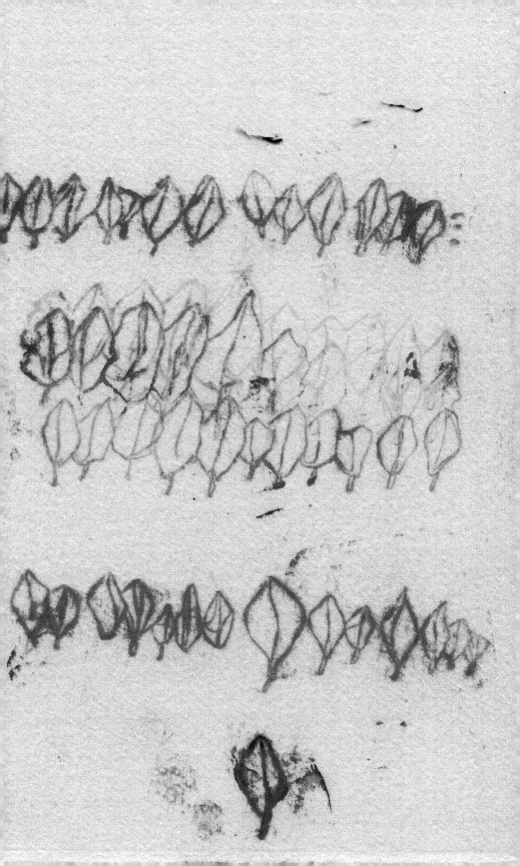

What a Mother Does
What a Mother does
is make crepes
and pizza for
those who
are hungry,
put diapers
onesies,
leggings, and
cardigans on
those who
are naked, and
give vitamin c
drops and tissues to
those who
are sick.

What Sara Taught Me
How the Mother feels
about rests and breaks,
how sometimes She binge
watches sunsets and flowers.

The Napping Place
Hers is a napping place.
You can rest here.

The Mother Embodies Her Mother

The Mother embodies
Her Mother while
She combs
Her daughter's
hair,
nearly
Rapunzel-length
long and
tangled, while
Her daughter
pleads,
Comb it
carefully.

She holds sprays
and wide tooth comb
and tries.
(She really tries.)
But sometimes
it still hurts.

Things She Hopes for Her Daughters

That they don't hate their curly
(or straight, or wavy)
hair,
or their aquiline
(or big, or small)
noses
or their too thin
(or too thick)
bodies,
or themselves.

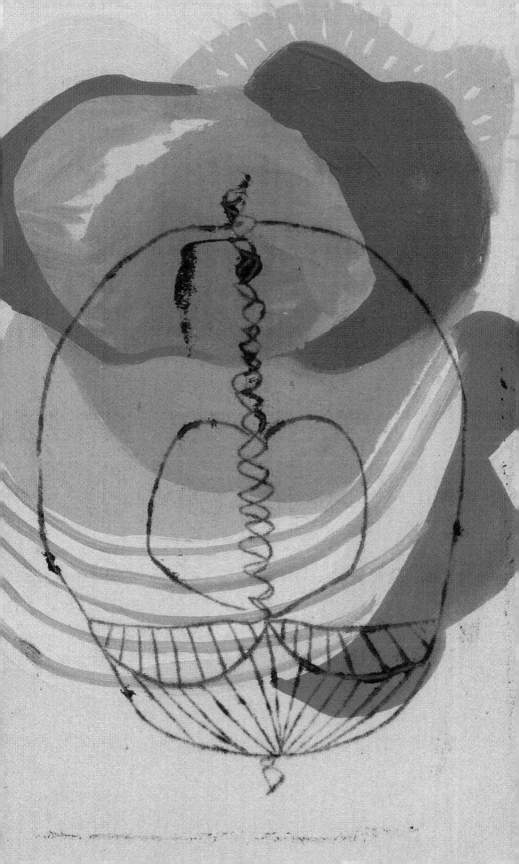

The Mother Loves the World
She loves the world.
She loves the whole
damn world.

As C told me,
Heavenly Mother is
a *mother to us—*
a *mother to us all.*

Design Mom
She has more than
seven children,
changes Her
hair and clothes
with the seasons,
reds, and oranges,
and yellows in fall,
silver and white
in winter, soft green
and pinks in spring,
and a handsome
home She calls
the world. She
will give you
a tour.

What Else Maggie Taught Me
The Mother wants us to love the world
because She made it,
because She brought us here.

FHE
Monday evenings,
She looks each person
in the eye,
shakes their hand
and says,
*Welcome to Family
Home Evening.*

What Zena Taught Me
There is a grandma God,
fierce and tiny,
who wears red,
drinks cocoa daily,
plants avocado
and lemon trees,
makes cheese
sandwiches,
and paints the
ocean blue.

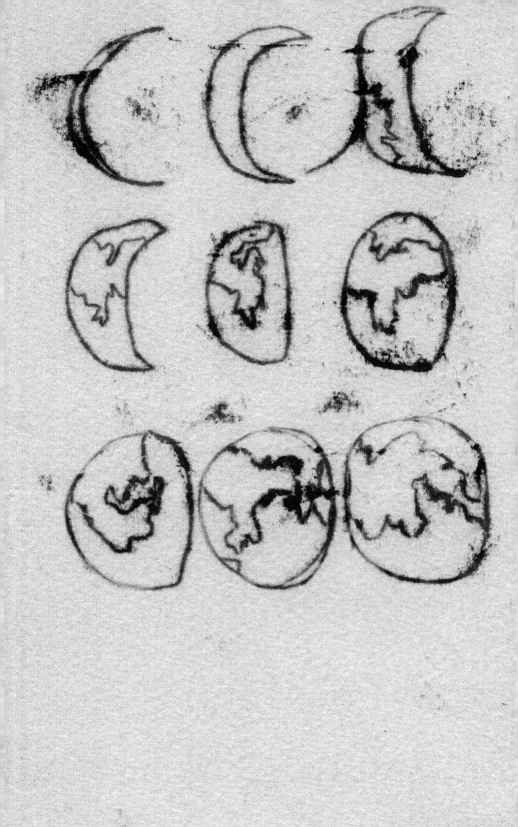

Unraveling
The Mother too,
unravels, thread
and heart pulled
from aching, grief,
or sorrow until
there is nothing
woven. Until,
She picks
up Her needles
and knits
again.

Mother Winter
Mother Winter
returns to
Herself, walks
slow steps, sips
slow sips
(lavender lemonade
tea with honey), breathes
cold breaths.

The Knitter
She doesn't mind
the weather.
She knits hearts,
and caps, and sweaters
for blustery days.

A Girl
On the ferry today,
C said,
The water has
blue hair, black
shoes, and a green
sweater, but
the water is
a Girl.

After the ferry,
C passed a
replica of the
statue of Liberty
and said,
That's the Mom
with Her book.

Like Lady Liberty

Like Lady Liberty,
The Mother faces
eastward and to
the south. She
stands straight
and tall, and
wears a crown
with seven spikes
for wholeness,
and sunbeams,
and continents,
and great rivers,
and gentle reminders
that all people are
Her people.
She holds a light
and book
and welcomes.

A Duet

A chorus, sometimes
in unison, sometimes
not, on New York City
sidewalk, yellow cabs,
food stands, lamb
and rice gyros, *Mama*
Mama
Mama
Mama
Mama
Mama.

On the Third Day of School
Cora told me,
All of the kids
missed their
Mommy.
They always
do.

The Linguist
She understands the
cries of Her children:
Ahm, Matka,
Mor, Móðir,
Mãe, Moer,
Máthair, Mère,
Mutter, Mum,
Mati, Majka,
Madre, Mamma,
Okaasan, Mūkīn,
Ibu, Mat',
Mami, Mzazi,
Mommy,
more.

She Knows it By Heart

Her seat of memory
is in Her heart.
She carries all of the
alphabets of the world,
the motions of the stars
and suns, the first time
a baby laughed and cried,
the first time She did.

God Talks to My Daughter, Again

She:
I want to hear your heart.

C:
I think it's broken. I can't hear anything.

The God Who Weeps

The Mother cries at commercials
She doesn't know are commercials,
She cries at every birth and every death.
She will cry at yours and mine.
She cries at the gentleness and cruelty
of others, at others' hurts, others' loneliness,
others' hopes, others' tries.
She cries at a particularly beautiful piece
of artwork, including sometimes Her own,
the way She quilts the sky in pinks and blues,
in purples and oranges, in hazy grays.
She cries at the way the trees look when
Her Son's light leaves for the night
and the gradual darkening, before.
She cries at track meets, when someone
breaks a record or runs a particularly
glorious race, and when someone
doesn't, but keeps going.

The Mother Cried Power
The Mother cried power,
cried anger,
cried sorrow,
cried tired,
cried empathy,
cried hunger,
cried naked,
cried lonely,
cried houseless,
cried gentleness,
cried kindness,
cried redemption,
cried hope,
cried charity,
cried joy.

What Laurel Taught Me
When asked,
She answers
Her anger
comes in
waves,
then pauses:
Be patient with
your anger.

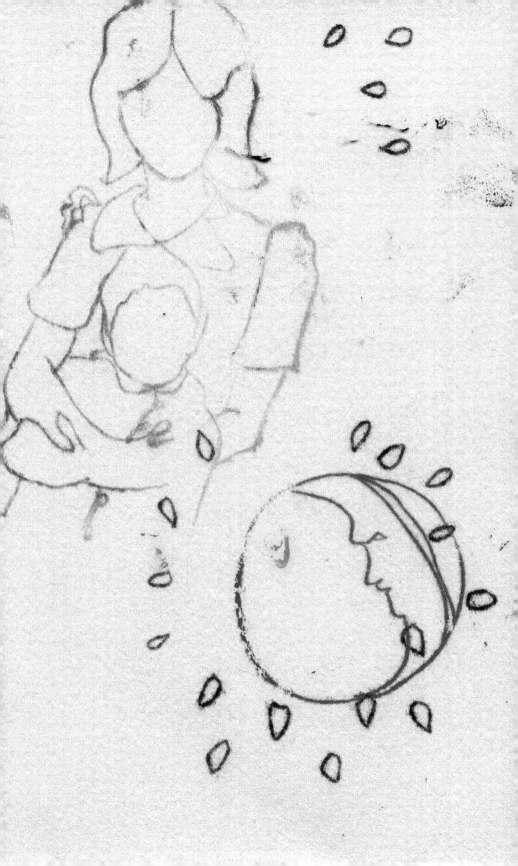

On Female Anger
The Mother consoles
Her daughters:
It's ok to scream.
Sometimes screaming
is required.

What Rebecca Ann Taught Me
One time, in the temple,
after sitting, and feeling,
and listening, and wondering
about joy and rage
a quietness spoke back.
It said, *He said:*
Don't worry about them.
Come talk to me for a bit.
You are your Mother's daughter.
That rage is Hers. And now it's yours.
Crying came, and a moment
of connection to Her—
a lifted veil.

What Te Fiti Taught Me
The Mother does not always
need to talk.
Sometimes She
just offers gifts,
forgiveness,
with an
open palm.

What the Women of Moana Taught Me
Moana, who heard
the voice of the ocean
and herself, who carried
her grandmother's stories
and the goddess's heart;

her mother, who packed quietly
and encouraged quietly;

her grandmother, who spoke loudly
and laughed loudly, who danced
and carried stories in her heart
and saw inside her granddaughter's;

Te Kã, who felt rage
appropriate for having
Her heart clawed out
and taken;

Te Fiti, who healed,
who found herself again
with help, who grew
green leaves,
and gave,
and forgave.

Climbing Mother

She is a ladder,
and a chair, and
a bed, and a pillow,
and a tightrope
walker, and a drinking
fountain for
Her children
and more than
all of those
together,

and more still;
She is a woman
and a God.

What the Exponent Taught Me

The Mother honors
women's stories and
women's voices.
She holds them
to Her ear, writes
them down (on leaves,
on stones, in rivers)
then sends
them off on
angel's wings.

Without a Microphone

Without a microphone,
Hers is a soft voice.
She is speaking straining
throat muscles trying
to make Herself heard.
For the people in the
back and middle,
She says, *There are
still seats at the front
if you can't hear.
You can come
closer.*
She talks as loud
as She can.

The Unheard Mother

The unheard Mother
hears mothers,
as well as women
who are not yet,
nor ever will
be mothers
(by chance
or choice).
She knows their
individual and
collective aches,
wants, rest,
joy, intelligence,
trauma, screaming,
as well as their
profound and utter
value,
each one
as whole,
as She.
She bids us,
Hear them.

She Hears

She hears women's silent prayer,
Can I nurture this life inside me?
Can I let it grow?
She understands when the
answer is No.

Vision of All
The Mother still
remembers
the moment
the Messenger
first said,
Look—

the views from
mountaintops, and
trees, and birds' eyes
that zoomed in and
in until She could
see the heart of
humanity, the hearts of
humans.

How Heavens Weep
She wept tears
as rain on mountains,
water swept
upward with nowhere
else to go, air
cooled, vapor
condensed, and
cloud formed
pouring down
as sobs too
heavy for the
sky.

Why Heavens Weep
It started with
looking—She saw
how cold
our hearts are,
how hard it is
for us to love.
She saw
that we
would hurt.

What Lisa Taught Me
No member of the
body of Christ
is expendable.
The Mother weeps
over every loss,
every wound.
She feels each
one.

What Joe and Gina Taught Me
In less desperate times,
God could stay up in heaven.
That was fine with me.
In more desperate times,
She comes down.
In more desperate times,
She leaves Her throne,
the Goddess of Earth
at the very heartbeat
of creation.

Did Not Doubt
They had been taught
by their Mother—
how to be carried,
how to drink milk and
eat honey, how to speak
in the language of Her
tongue, and how if
they did not doubt,
God would deliver them.
They did not doubt
Her.

Eleven

A girl with a
number for a
name, who knew
only a Papa,
asked adamant,
*Do I have a
mama?*
then whispered
low and long,
Mama.

Prodigal Daughter

The lost daughter woke up
and returned to herself,
and determined she no
longer wanted to be lost,
and determined to
return to her Mother.

When she was still very
far, her Mother saw her
and had compassion
and dropped everything
She was carrying—Her
golden weaving and grief—
and ran to her, Her precious
daughter now found,
and threw herself into
her arms and kissed her

The Woman With Outstretched Arms

The Mother is a woman
with outstretched arms.
All day long, She wants
to welcome us. All day long
She wants us to run to Her.

The Women at the Well

She is with the women at the well,
with Hagar, with Rebecca, with Rachel,
with the woman whose name
we don't know, who talked with Jesus.
She is with Jesus.
She is in the well,
in the water and the stone,
in the earthy coldness and depth,
the life-giving.
She is in the thirst
and the quenching of the thirst.
She is in the giving and receiving
and meeting.
She gives us drink
wellspring willingly.
Still, we must
dip or pulley.

Blood Issues
The Mother knows
about blood issues
meant to follow the
moon, and a woman
whose blood lasted
twelve years. She
witnessed the woman
in crowds for those
long years, searching
quiet, waiting quiet, faith
quiet, until touching hems
quiet, healing quiet, and
being seen by Her son,
loud.

Our God
She is our God,
our mother's/
sister's/niece's/
daughter's/
granddaughter's
God. She holds
Her almighty hands
open before Her.

Jane

She walked with Jane
bare feet across
miles and state
lines, to a place
that wasn't quite
Zion, but tried.
She wept with her
when she cried that
the folks have all gone
and got themselves
homes but she *got*
none, and when
Joseph and Emma
offered theirs.
She watched her
hungry for bread,
give half of her flour
to feed others.
She heard her ask
Is there no blessing
for me? and whispered
back, *There is. There is.*

Emma
She watched Emma
pack her cart again,
build a home, lose
a home, welcome
strangers, share
her husband—willingly
and unwillingly—
care for children
and patients,
bury her own babies,
preside as president,
speak wise words,
lay hands on heads,
write wise words,
bless herself,
and stay.

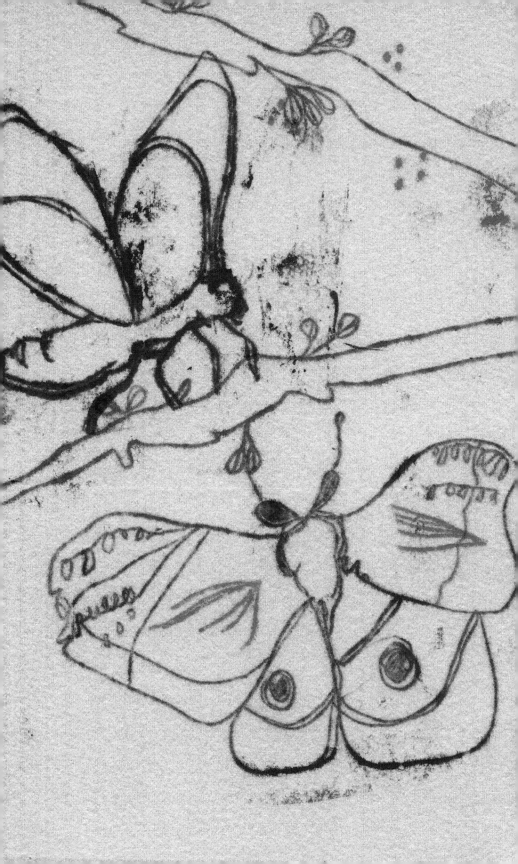

Hewed Out
The Mother built
Her house.
She hewed out
Her seven pillars—
wisdom, love,
faith, mercy,
joy, sorrow,
hope.
She furnished
Her table–
with grapes,
cheese, bread,
olives.
She cried
on mountaintops
and rooftops.

Maman
I see Her—
Louise's spider
Mother, standing
18 feet tall
from steel or flesh,
a repairer of things
that are broken,
a weaver of river
warmed tapestries
and girls, of stories,
and stars, and
songs, and webs
made whole.

What Louise Taught Me

Louise whispered past time
and space and her own
death that when spiders and
Mothers lose Their home—
when someone breaks it—
They don't get mad,
They just build
again.

Swaying Woman

I see Her in women
who have held babies
and swayed shopping carts
without babies,
in Aimee, Caroline,
my mother, and me.

A House

She is a house,
a temple unto
Herself,
a house that knows
She is
a house.

Grandmother

Tom told us about
Grandmother, his
affectionate name
for his affectionate
temple in Kirtland,
built as much with faith
and hope as hands;
his stories punctuated
with, *My people, my
people*, and distinctions
between new railing
alongside the original
we could not touch—
That's Grandmother.

What Terry Taught Me

The Earth and Her
trees are suffering.
We are hurting Them.
They whisper,
We are struggling.
We're not thirsty,
we're dying.
Our roots are being crushed.
We can hear Them if
we listen.

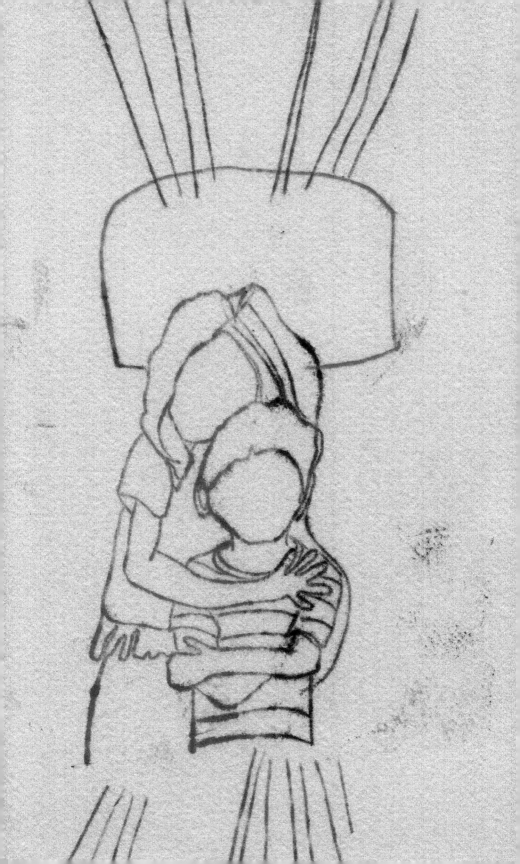

Like TTW
Does She pray to
the birds?
Do they teach Her
how to listen?

To Tree
Heavenly Mother speaks to tree;
tree speaks to stone;
stone speaks to water;
water speaks to earth;
earth speaks to sky;
sky speaks to bird;
bird speaks to Heavenly Mother;
who speaks to tree.

What the Mother Prays To
The Mother prays to
birds of all kind, and
trees, and flowers.
She prays to rivers,
calm or quick, to
oceans' opening.
She prays to beginnings, to
endings, and sometimes
even to middles.
She prays to me, to
you. But most of all,
She prays to
Herself.

Hub Tree

The Mother tree
speaks and recognizes
Her kin, like
a mama grizzly
her cubs.

She nurtures Her
seedlings in
their understory,
sending nutrients
below and
hugging Her
roots in tight
so Her children's
roots can grow.

When She is hurt
or almost dead, She
sends messages
below, wisdom
for Her next
generation of
seedlings.

Rooted
The Mother
stands rooted
welcoming,
but sends
Her shoots into
the world—
stems/leaves/
tenderness/
buds/flowers/
empathy/
nuts/fruits/
branches/
wisdom.

What Page Taught Me
The Mother knows
Her hills and
walks them,
bending down to
pick up
a leaf here,
a twig there,
a feather.
She opens
antique chests and
drawers,
bending down to
gather tools from
women come before—
wax thread,
large-eye needles,
scissors, thimbles,
lace, buttons,
worn quilts, and
dresses.
She bundles,
and unbundles,
and bundles
again,
scraps
made sacred.

She Brave Woman

The Mother hangs
homemade banners in
homemade woods
for students
and strollers
to pass,
reminding
Her children to
BE BRAVE.

Hide-and-Seek

The Mother and I play
hide-and-seek.
I count loudly
while She runs
to hide, *One, two,*
three, four, five, six,
seven, eight, nine,
ten. Then, *Ready*
or not, here I come!
And I am ready
to find Her,
to at least begin
looking.

Hide-and-Seek II

After long search,
I give up. I yell,
Olly olly oxen free.
I yell, *You can come*
out now.
You won.

Hide-and-Seek III

The Mother and I don't play
hide-and-seek anymore.
She said we grew too old
to hide from one another.
Soon we gave up on hiding
altogether. Now we lay
bare—our fear and
courage, our sorrow and
joy, our secrets and shame,
our lost loves and grief,
our hopes and belief.

Her Hands are Open

The Mother dreamt
of eternal rest
once, or twice, or three
thousand times.
She understands
and holds Her hands
out to those
who seek it.

Out of the Blue

Out of the blue, Cora asked me,
*What's God's job and did He
get married?* Out of the blue I
answered, *What do you think
God's job is? I think God is
an artist. And yes. Our Mama.*

She Casts the First and Last Stones

The Mother casts stones
in bronze, and gold, and
aged green paint to give
to Her grandchildren.
They are not for throwing.

What Caitlin and Sarah Taught Me

The Mother is a woman
with deep roots
and firm branches.
She nurtures yellow light,
green growth, and children.
She's a painter, a carver,
and printer.
She has large hands that work.

The Artist
She knows
stained glass
is made by
breaking and
then melding
new.

She practices
tapping.

The Composer
The Mother gathers notes
from the four corners of
the earth, from bugs and
birds; leaves being whisked
by wind; rivers running
into oceans; the crash of
waves those oceans make;
children giggling; lovers
singing, or sighing, or crying;
the softest sound of one intake
of breath; kissing.

What Nate Taught Me
She made Hildegard wild with song and fire.
She twined Bach in revolving heavens of counterpoint.
She wrestled with Beethoven until he became
mighty and new and sorrowful.
She begged Cage to respect silence and sound,
and She inspired Clara Schuman, too. She sang
with Barbara Strozzi. She guided Sofia
Gubaidulina into frightful intensities, and gave
Nadia Boulanger her utter trust.
They know how to listen.

What Shaura Taught Me
To hear Her, we must
listen to the low notes.

Hearing Across
I heard my baby and
husband laugh
from the bathtub
on a day that
they weren't home—
hearing across
memories.
Sometimes, I can
almost hear
my Mother.

I am Here
She heard Her
children volunteer
themselves over
and over, saying
Here am I, send me.
She pleaded to go
in their stead
shouting, *I AM HERE!*

Alpha and Omega
The Mother is a small seed,
a beginning and ending,
hallowed out and cracked
open ready to grow.

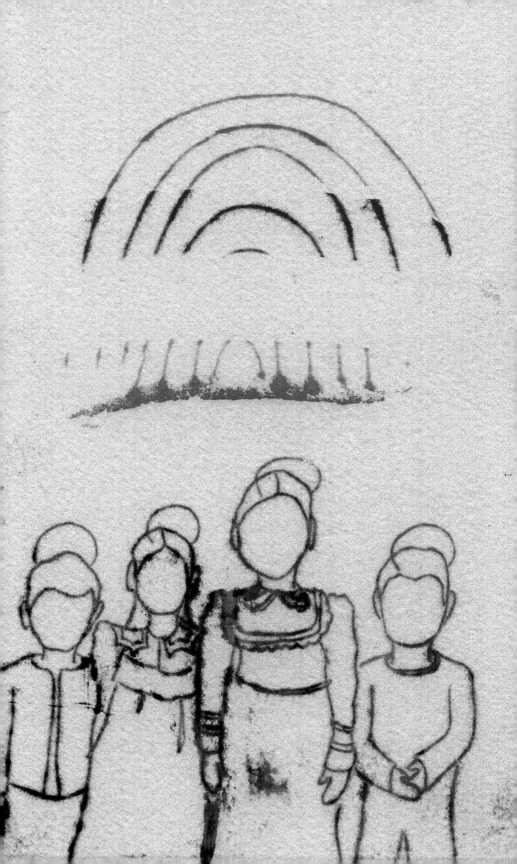

Where She Carries
She carries Her stress
in Her left shoulder, Her
lament for Her brother
in Her neck, Her inability
to sleep in Her lower back,
Her remembrance that some
live in the world without
grandparents, without parents,
in Her upper back, Her nostalgia
for childhood in Her spine,
Her grief at the hatred in the world
in her hands, missing every bike
She ever owned in Her right knee,
Her inability to run the distances
She used to in Her shins, Her
longing for lost lovers
in Her lungs, Her emptiness
in Her womb, Her loneliness
in Her heart.

When Things Break

When things break,
there are sharp edges,
pieces to sweep from off the floor,
shards that can cut you.

Things break. You get cut.
There are losses.

The Mother binds your wounds,
salvages what can be salvaged
and holds the dust pan
for your broom.

Kintsugi

She knows what
to do with shattered
vessels(hearts), how
to piece them back
together carefully
and line the cracks
with gold.

The Laughing God
Heavenly Mother can
laugh and weep
at the same time
without cheating
either. She is the
Laughing God
as much as the
Weeping one—
Her laughter and
tears overspilling
what cannot be
contained. They
are where words
are not enough.

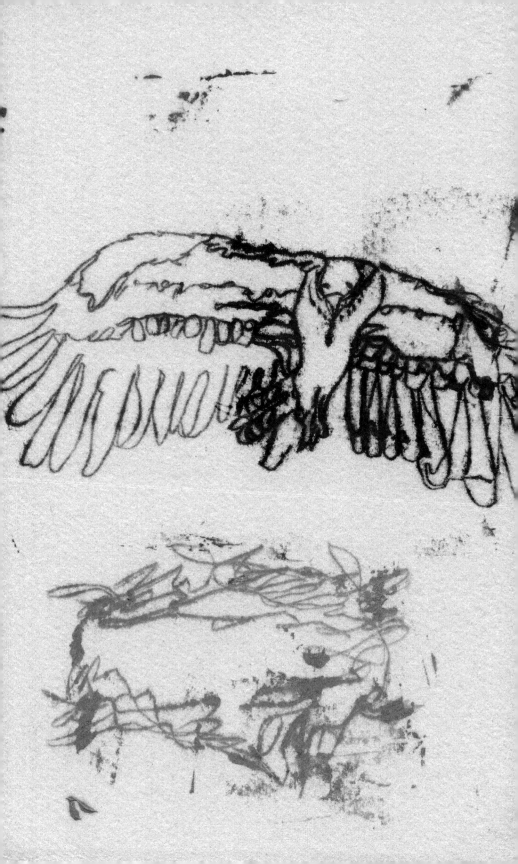

My Daughter Talks to the Moon
My daughter talks to the Moon,
calling out, *Hi, Girl Moon. Hi.*
The Moon talks to my daughter
by shining gentle, silver light,
Hi girl. Hi.

Moon Mother
Each night,
She wrestles the
light from the
darkness,
and each night,
She wins.

Each night
She cries for
Her children
in their darkness,
and each night
She holds them
tightly so that
they can win.

What Paul Taught Me
No border
can separate us
from Her love,
not even ones
separating countries
and earth mothers
from earth babies—
not even those.

Other Things that Will Not Separate us from Her Love:
Being born, being sad, being mad,
being scared, being hurt, being hungry,
being naked, being lonely, being addicted,
being poor, being single, being married,
being childless, being divorced,
being widowed, being dead.

Ninety-nine is not Forever
My mother thought
her own mother would
live forever.
Don't we all?

When My Grandmother Was Dying
When my grandmother
was dying in California,
I was wearing her coat
in New York, and the one
we share as Mother
was holding us both.

To Dress Her Body

I.
Before I drove to my
granny Billie's empty home,
my mom asked if I wanted
to go to the funeral home
to dress her body. I surprised
myself by saying yes. I
don't remember very much,
but do remember stretching
slightly too small shoes on
slightly too large feet
and feeling grateful.

II.
After I drove to my
grandma Zena's still full (of
cousin and grandchildren) home,
my mom asked the question
she asked me before: did I want
to go to the funeral home?
Again, I answered yes.
Again, I stretched shoes on stiff,
statuesque feet,
then I held my grandmother's
head in my hands and kissed
her hair and blessed her.

Worth Saving
The Mother loves us
in our brokenness,
our tenderness,
our fragility, and
vulnerability.
She's not afraid
of our screaming
sobbing, lip quivering
shaking. She knows
that just because
we can get hurt
does not mean
that we are not
worth saving.

What Jason Taught Me
The Mother is my
most faithful friend.
She has always
walked with me
through everything
and always will.

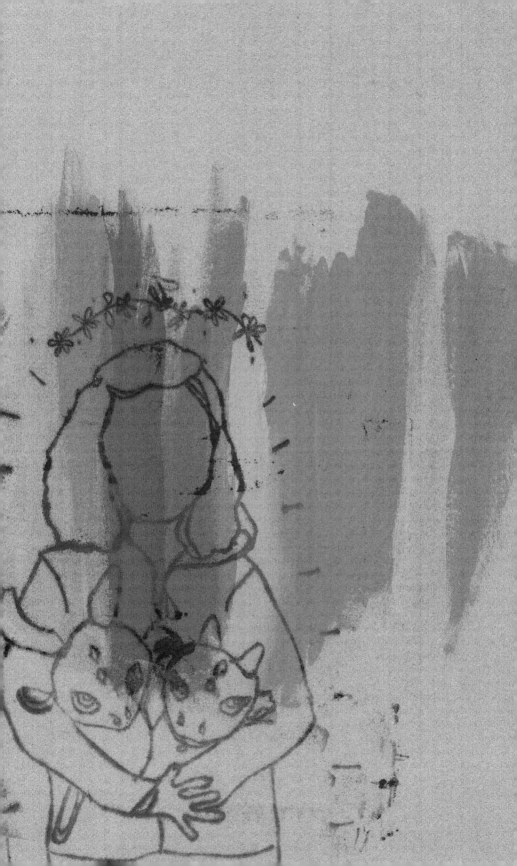

The Inner Vessel
She is cleansing
the inner vessel,
through tears,
through gentleness,
through patience,
through trying,
through loving anyway,
living anyway,
through grace,
wide enough
for me.

What Else Jason Taught Me
The Mother walks with us
on hard roads
and gentle roads.
She loves us that much
and Her legs are strong.
She does not
get weary.

She knows how
deeply the world
hurts all of us.
We are in the
best hands.

Her Body
Her body will
carry her
through grief,
through life,
through birth,
and giving birth.

Hyrum Dead/Jesus Dead
I know what it
is like to have
a brother, the
oldest son.
She knows what it
is like to have
a son, the
oldest brother.
We both know what it
is like to lose
him/them.
Hyrum dead.
Jesus dead.

The Most Moved Mover
It felt brave, at first
for Her to be so vulnerable.
Then it became a matter
of survival.

I Need God to Talk to My Brother

I need God
to talk
to my brother,
to say, *Hi,*
to say, *I love you,*
to say, *Your sister*
loves you,
to say, *Welcome*
Home.

What Rebecca Taught Me

After grief of all kinds, let
cold rain soak into your
cold skin, let your feet touch
the earth, bare. The Mother's
body can carry it.
It is big enough.

The Writing After the Disaster
The Mother sits with
you while you write
after the disaster,
after the divorce,
the first thought
of divorce,
after the death,
the first thought
of death,
after the car accident,
the first thought
of car accidents,
after the birth,
the first thought
of birth.

The Mother Carries Tissue
She wipes
away tears
from off
all faces.

And Grace
The Mother knows
the oldest song that
was ever sung, the
one that shaped the
world, and the new
song that will be sung
together, of Zion, and
redemption, and grace.

What Else Page Taught Me
The Mother bundles—

books,
pages bound
with careful thread;

bodies, flesh sewn
after birth and
veils torn
open;

babies, in
soft swaddles;

children, in cozy
coats and mittens;

partners, to each
other, parents to
children, sibling to
sibling

in ties that
bind with rings
and words—
seals, to each
other and to

Her.

Bloomsbury
She is my
Bloomsbury,
my perfect place—
the one not on any map,
that must be painted.

My Daughter Teaches Me Where the Map Is
I found my daughter
on my bed, donning
yellow flower leggings
and a BYU cheerleading
outfit, resting my own
copy of *Mother's Milk*
on her knees, open
with pen in hand.
She drew on every page—
a face here, a line,
a squiggle—and on the
title page, her largest work.
Your book is a map now,
to find our way to our old home.
It's everyone's map!

What the Raven-haired Mother Taught Me
On sheaves of paper,
and bird's wings,
and maps and maps,
She is here.
She is here.
She is here.
And she was.
The daughter was.

The Girl Who Was the Moon
She knows that there are some
who hold out their hands
to the moon and gather its sticky
light, like honey on their fingertips
and drink. And then there's Her,
who was the moon.

What the Raven-haired Daughter Taught Me
In her private journal,
and her private heart,
and maps and maps,
She is here.
She is here.
She is here.
And she was.
The Mother was.

Moonbeam
The Son may want
me for a sunbeam
but the Mother wants
me for a moonbeam
to shine when it's
most dark,
gently enough to
not hurt human eyes,
brightly enough to
lend hope.

Raw Honey
She is raw honey,
sweet, but not
saccharine, complicated
with tones of clover
and honeysuckle,
made by the generosity
of flowers and the work
of bees.
Found locally,
can strengthen
your immunity,
can heal you
if you let it.

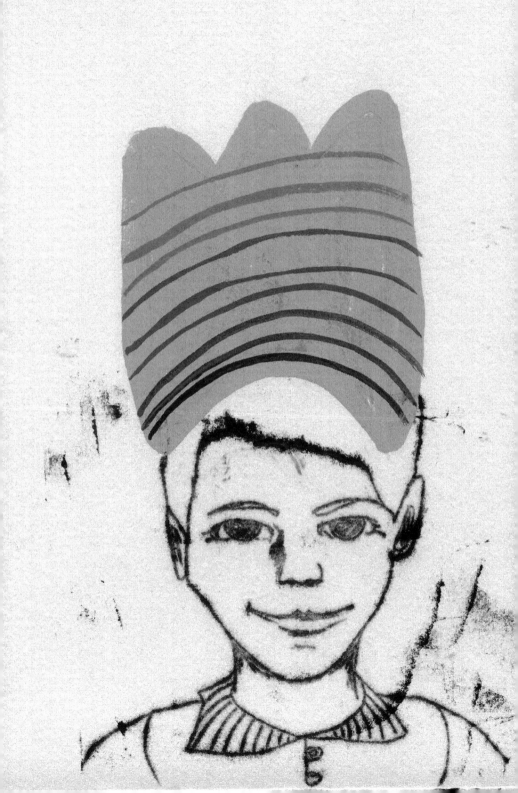

Queen Bee

When the Queen Bee is gone,
the city stops. The young
are forgotten; the old
wander, lost, looking
for their Mother. Some
stay in the hive and others
without. Workers stop
working; foragers stop
foraging. (They do not
visit the flowers, though
they be there in summer's
bloom.) Guards leave
their posts. Marauders
sweep in, stealing honey.
The inhabitants die
of sorrow.

Lament

Gina knows the Mother,
knows the women
standing outside gates
crying, lamenting across
large walls.
She says, *Name it.*
Name it. Again and
again and again.
Name the Mother.
Name the lament.
Name the wall.
Wail.
Say it until they
can't ignore it.
Until they listen.

My Sorrow

My sorrow fills
the oceans—
the Pacific first
bleeding into
the Atlantic, then
the Indian, then
the Arctic.
It's ok.
My Mother's filled
them first.

Yokes

My yoke is heavy
and my burden
is heavy, but
the Mother has
been around
a long time.
She can help
carry it, with Christ.
Their yokes and
burdens are light
and light.

After Moving to China

After moving to China
I said I think of God
as a Mother. A woman
said, *Really? I think of Her*
as saving people from the sea
and told me about Mazu,
a real person who rescued
sailors from shipwreck
and storm and is thought
to be the Chinese goddess
of the sea.

Months later I stood on
an island near Hong Kong
with another woman.
She said that all of
the temples on her island
are for female deities
and that they're all active.
She pointed to one that
was for fertility and another
for protection from the sea:
She takes care of the sailors.

What Dar Taught Me

She is the welcome
home from the ocean,
the towel you don't
have to share with your
sister, the still hot shower
you're second in line for,
the sand rinsing off of
your body.

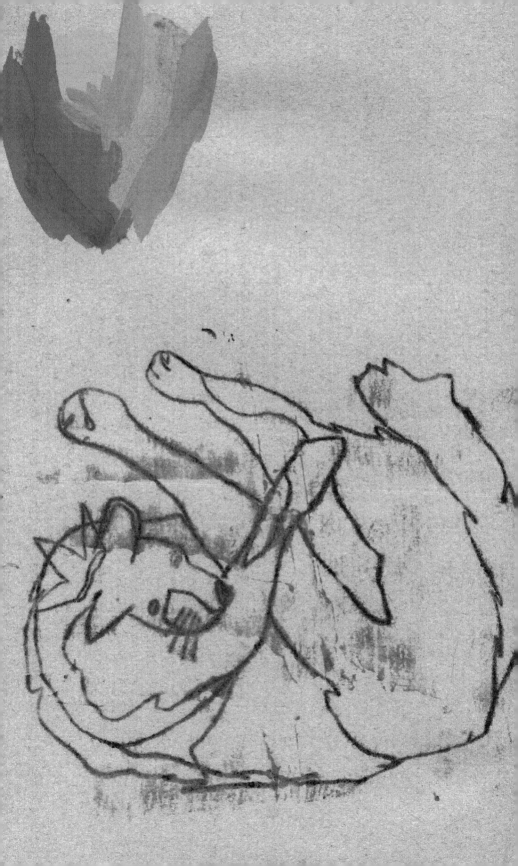

What Ariel Taught Me
You were given
your Mother's voice.
Don't bargain it away
so easily,
not even for
a pair of legs.

Flora, Fauna, and Merryweather
If Flora gave Aurora
the gift of beauty,
and Fauna the gift
of song, before
Maleficent gave
the gift of death
(which Merryweather
softened to the gift
of sleep), the true
Godmother would
have given the gift
of charity, or perhaps
wisdom.

What Little Zina Taught Me
God is a woman,
is good,
is real,
loves you,
is a mother.

God is not
patriarchy.
You can cross
it out.

Faith
She believes in us
first, before
She asks us
to believe in Her
and in Her son.
She sees our
unseen hearts.
They give Her
faith.

Divine Nature

Fully half of our
divine nature and
destiny comes
from Her. She
is a glorious,
exalted, noble
one.

Individual Worth

The Mother is whole
unto Herself, just
like Her daughters.
She and they are
worthy. She and
they are worth
everything.

Knowledge

She reminds gently,
you can take
knowledge
with you.
You can take
Wisdom
with you.

Choice and Accountability

It may be said, that the Mother
is an open theist and that
Hers is a freedom project;
She is committed to our
agency, to our choosing;
even when it hurts Her,
even when it hurts us.
Her love is Her power.

Good Works
The Mother believes
in doing good, in pure
religion—to visit the
parentless and widows
in their affliction—but
it doesn't save us.
(We still need Jesus.)

Integrity
The Mother's is
an intensely
focused heart,
brave and pure,
committed to
Herself.

Virtue
She knows virtue is
something deep
in us. It isn't easily
taken or untaken.

Dinah
Her name means
divine justice,
matched only by
Her divine mercy.

The Judge
The Judge
of the universe
sometimes goes
by *Mommy*,
loves burritos,
bingeing human
TV shows, and
staying impartial.

What Ruth Taught Me
The Mother dissents
and sometimes
She doesn't.

New Moon
She is a moon
without a moon,
the holding place
for the moon,
the making room
for the moon.
She is the hope
of a moon, of
a new light,
a new month,
beckoning us:
Her light will
come back.

Moonstone
Carved into
granite in holy
places, She
represents
the days, and
weeks, and
months, and
cycles that
guide us,
the light that
grows and dims
and grows, the
ocean that pulls
and wavers, the
life it gives that
continues.

The Hour of Land
The Mother is
reclaiming Her
hour, of land,
of sky, of sea,
Her hour of place
and the holding
of place. She
knows those
hours are sacred.

I Was Home
Who does he look for
in the morning
when he can't
find his Mother?
His Aunt?
His Grandmother?

He didn't come
to my door.
He didn't climb
in my bed.
He didn't know
I was home.

Peeling Back the Veil

I opened the door
because he was lonely
without you.
I opened the door
so he could find
you.

My Son

He finds me
each day,
my Sun.
We rise
together.

Unveiled

The Mother
unveils her
face and will
not take it up
again—Her Son
tore it, anyway.
She prefers easy
breathing, and
speaking, and
seeing. She will
not be muffled
anymore, nor
hidden. When
She hearkens
She does so to
Herself.

A Great Wonder

John saw Her,
a great wonder
in heaven, a
woman wearing
the sun and a
crown with twelve
stars, the moon
resting under Her
feet. He heard Her
cry in childbirth,
travailing to
deliver Herself.

Clothed
The Mother wears
strength and dignity
as garments and
laughs without being
afraid of what's
to come.

The Queen of Heaven
The Queen of Heaven whispers,
Pawns can become queens
if they travel far enough.
And they can, however
slowly they are first required
to move, however unimportant
and disposable they are deemed.
They can have the greatest
movement, exceeding even
the King.

Crowns
The Mother has seven
crowns. She knows
which one to wear:
Monday figs, Tuesday
thistles, Wednesday
flowers, Thursday stars,
Friday moons, Saturday
suns, Sunday songs.

The High Priestess
Eliza was called after Her,
Zion's poetess, prophetess,
priestess, having authority.

The Daughters of Miriam
She brought the daughters of
Miriam to the door of the temple
and washed them with water,
and dressed Miriam in the
holy garments, and anointed her,
and sanctified her; that she may
minister to Her in the priestess's office.

Zelophehad's Daughters
The Mother stood with
Zelophehad's daughters
as they stood before
Moses, and Eleazar,
and princes, and the
whole congregation
as they demanded a
possession of their
inheritance, a right
their tradition denied
them, but their God
wanted to give them,
their Mother wanted
to give them.

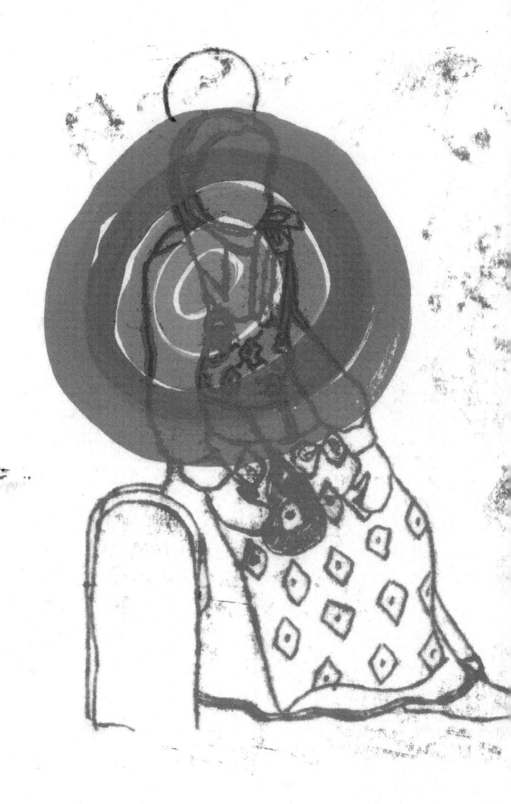

In My Mother's House

In my Mother's house
are many other houses
as big or as small
as we like. Jesus
went to prepare
one for you, and
you, and you, and
me.

Wild Flock

We are Her
wild flock
that does not
have to be good,
but instead
has to love, and
love, and love,
and trust that
even in our listening
and telling of despair
and loneliness
we belong
to Her.

Pilgrimage
The Mother
understands
pilgrims leaving
home, seeking
refuge in further
light and knowledge
and souls who
share the way.
She journeyed
first.

Mother Maple
The Mother is beautiful.
She reflects Her age and
pain, Her striving to reach
toward the Sun, to live through
long winters, and to have deep
roots and strong branches.
She gives us sap, sweet
as honey.

Second Miracle
The Mother's first miracle was
turning water into milk.
Her second was
turning thistles into figs,
words into poems,
hunger into nourishment.

Names
Defiantly,
I'm not only good
at naming
Myself
and I know
all of the names
so quickly.

Three
My daughter tries on different
names, insists they're hers—
Anna, Elsa, Rapunzel, Belle, Peg,
Cat, Ariel, Doc McStuffins, Mama—
until she casts them off, picks
her own name from off the floor,
says, *Cora,* then, *I changed back into*
myself.

My daughter mourns the loss of
balloons, insists I blow them up
again–torn latex, green polka dots—
until I say I can't, and she casts the
scraps off on the floor, wraps
tiny arms around me and
sobs, *But it was so*
beautiful.

I Gave Her a Name

I gave Her a name
and then another
and another, letting
old names fall to the
floor when they were
past fitting.
She gave me names,
words, floors, myself,
balloons, beauty, scraps,
everything.

Alma

One of Her names
is Alma. She is
every girl in
every chapter
of the history
of love, of life.

Billie

She is young and old
at the same time—
a quiet blue-eyed,
brown-haired baby
born just after loss
and a brown-eyed,
white-haired woman
with a deep voice, lost
Herself to us, to earth,
but not to everyone
to heaven.

Open-Handed

Her name is Open-
Handed. She makes
a hundred years of
winter on a summer's
day; brings golden
sunlight to winter;
calls new trees out
of the earth that bear
snow white fruit; heals
holes in mountain sides;
bestows names; and
changes silver to gold
in Her hands.

The Name I Call Her

The name I call Her,
I keep in my heart
or in my palm—
a white stone.

White Fruit
Look—
A tree,
a beautiful tree,
the most
beautiful tree,
the most snow
white,
the most
precious.

Your father tasted
its fruit. Remember
how it made
him happy?
It's the most sweet,
the most desirable.

Look—
A woman.
She is
the most
beautiful.
The most
precious.

Look[feel]—
God's love.
the most
beautiful.
The most
precious.

The woman,
again.
She is the mother of
the son of
God.
Look—
a child in
her arms.

Listen—
the meaning of the tree?
It's His other Mother.
Look at
Her fruits—
the love
of God.
The most
precious.
The most
joyous to
the soul.

Abish
One woman
can have a vision
of her father
turn to the Lord
and hold her vision
quiet in her heart
for many years
until it's time
to run from house
to house
and change a kingdom.

What Sara Katherine Taught Me
The Baader-Meinhof
Phenomenon applies
to our Mother. After
you first have reason
to see Her, you see Her
everywhere,

in the faces of the
old, the middle-aged,
and very young,

in freckles, in big
expressions and
small ones. In
quietness, and
fierceness, and
silliness,

She is there
waiting to
be seen.

The Mormon Women Project

The Mother believes
in the mission of the
Mormon Women Project.
She cherishes each interview
with Her daughters—each
voice, each brave path.

Mother in Heaven is for the ERA

Mother in Heaven is for the ERA and
for Mormons who are for the ERA.
(After all, they're everywhere.)
It's a pearl of great price
worth putting on a banner
and flying from the sky.

What's Her Name

She knows all of
the women's names
from history—from herstory—
that we should know,
as well as what it's like
to not have Her name
known.

Segullah
The Mother knows
we are treasure,
Her peculiar
people, Her
children.

Sister's Quorum
She sits at
the head
and talks
and listens.

Women's Work

Daughter,
you are elected
and ordained
to expound
and exhort—
the scriptures,
the church.
I elected you.

Daughter,
your time
is precious.
Give it to writing and
to learning
as much
as you can.
This is your work
(not cleaning,
not childcare).

Daughter,
you're a curator.
Gather hymns
in one place.
I will call it
good.
I will call it
delightful.

What Rachel Taught Me
The Mother looks forward
and back, ties knots in quilts,
has been a quilt, comforting
and keeping warm,
has worn a bonnet to
traverse mountains,
has been a mountain,
has been a sister
reaching her hand down
or up depending on
what's needed.

The Mother Reminds Us
The Mother reminds us of
the wisdom of cycles
in the earth, the seasons,
the moon, our bodies,
and ourselves.
She whispers when to
be slow and sleep
and when to speed
back up and wake,
when to grow and
die and grow
again.

Nesting

We nest into
each other
and back out
when we need to
be ourselves,
when we need to
let the past rest
and the future
dance.

We take the
shattered
glass trauma
out of our mouths
and die and
breathe again.

Mother Dough

She is Mother Dough,
Lievito Madre in Italian,
the ferment before
the ferment
that helps us rise,
and grows,
and grows,
and lives,
and lives.

What Henri Taught Me

The Mother is our sun
rising and setting
bringing new light,
new warmth, new
electricity, adding
color to our sky,
who sometimes has
to hide behind gray clouds.

When She Fell

When She walked
across the beam,
She remembered
to balance with arms
spread like wings,
to take careful steps
and brave ones,
and to get up
when She fell.

Glass or Flowers

Cora listened to her mother
read her poems about the Mother
out loud for hours, then said,
*I wonder if She actually wears
a dress made of glass or flowers.*

When Winter Still Sits in the Chair
The Mother teaches
bulbs how to spring
forth from cold
ground—crocuses,
daffodils, tulips.
Her heart bursts
blooming at their
hope brave
enough to act.

What Amanda Taught Me
Not every pregnancy
has a baby, and
not every Mother
has been pregnant.

We are woven
in miscarriages
and stillbirths,
in fosterings
and adoptions.

Phantom
She remembers
what it's like
to have life inside
Her womb
wiggling.
Sometimes
She still feels it,
phantom vibrations.

Her Womb
Her womb
has been empty
and full
and empty
and full
and empty
and full…

She Knows

She knows what
it's like to wake up
every morning
and ask, *Where
is my blood?*
She knows what
it's like to suspect
it's not coming.
She knows what
it's like to have
life inside Her
She's not quite
ready to have, that
She's scared to have.
She knows what
it's like to cry
and decide.

Notes from Her Journal

My body is shaping
up to be other than
it has been before.
It is more swollen.
More full.
On good days,
I think of it as my
soul swelling as
large as eternity,
my body and my heart.
On bad days,
I think of it as
simply swelling.

The Work I've Made

You are my daughter.
You are my son.
Look. I will show you
the work I've made
with my own hands,
but not all of it, because
my hands have not
stopped making,
and also my words,
because they
never stop.

YMF
You are the children of
your Mother who
is in heaven.
She makes Her
sun rise on the old
Mormon feminists
and the young
Mormon feminists
and those who aren't
Mormon and aren't feminist.
She sends Her rain
on the married and
unmarried, the stay-at-
home and the working.

She loves us all as flowers,
as more than flowers
all alike.
She knows we need
sun and rain both to grow
and thrive.

Queen Noor
The Queen of Heaven,
the Queen of Light
throws open
the windows and doors
to let the sun in.

Living With Her

She opens Her eyes
and I see
Cora,
Søren.

She opens Her ears
and I hear
laughing, crying,
singing.

She opens Her mouth
and I speak.

What Miranda and Calvin Taught Me

The Mother pleads
No one belongs here
more than you,
you who are sometimes
made to feel like
you don't belong
by fall(en) policies
and people.
She'll sit silently
beside you
on the pews
if you'll let Her
and understands
if you can't.

Thresholds
The Mother is at
the thresholds, the in
between places—
where forest stops
being forest,
where ocean stops
being ocean—
where they become
something different
so something different
can thrive.

What Kerry Taught Me
The Mother loves variety—
all of the messy flowers in
all of the messy gardens,
all of the spindly, leaning
trees in all of the spindly,
leaning forests, all of the
weird fish in all of the weird
deep and shallow seas,
all of the wild and tame
animals in all of the
wild and tame places
animals live, and all of the
seven colors in all of the
more than seven rainbows
and the more than seven
thousand colors without.
Don't ask Her to
choose a favorite.
She can't.
We're the ones who
pick and choose
and demand rigid
categories.

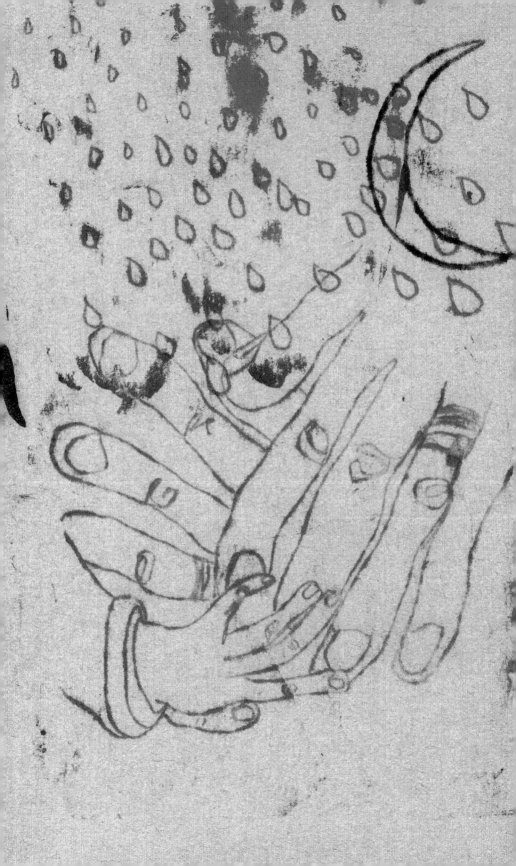

Chosen Names
She knows
the importance
of pronouns
and chosen names.

Hold On to These Names
Shaddai, Shekinah, Wisdom,
Asherah, Pneuma, Sophia,
Ruach, Hochma.

Sound Wisdom
Counsel is the Mother's,
and sound wisdom.
She is understanding;
She has strength.

Asherah
After Her temple burned
and Her trees burned,
after there were only
ashes, She planted a
seed to start again, and
watered it with Her
tears.

David Dying
I think that David
might be dying
(is that what
hospice means?)—
he, the person who
first asked me
to (re)search for the
Divine Feminine
in Mormonism,
to try.

When it's time,
may he go gentle
into Her good light.

What Martin Taught Me
A question I cannot
forget, ten years later:
*Cannot sons long
for their Mother?*

What Søren Taught Me
The Mother loves us
even when we name
ourselves *T-rex*
and roar loudly
in Her face
all day.

What Deidre Taught Me
The Mother knows
it's not selfish
to love Herself;
it's not selfish
to care for Herself.
(She would wear Millie's
mother's red dress.)
There are limits to
self-sacrifice.

Morning Sickness

What is there to say
about this, except to ask:
has She had it, too?
Did She stick Her head
fully out of taxi windows
trying to get
enough air?
Did She swallow ginger
tablets on ferry rides
and dowse Her forehead
with peppermint oil?
Did one of Her taxi drivers
stop by a woman selling
oranges on the side
of the road and persuade
her to offer one for free
to smell?
Did any of it help Her?
Will She help me?
Will She sit with me
when despite all my efforts
I throw up in Ziplock bags
taken out of pockets
just in time or on sidewalks
immediately after spilling
out of taxis?
Will She cry with me
when I cry
and my throat burns?

Was She ever more
absent to Her
other children
with whispered
apologies that *Mommy
doesn't feel well?*

Carry Me
Can you carry me
as I carry her?
Can you cradle me
as I cradle her
inside?

Homesick
Yesterday, crying in two
taxis in two foreign lands
wanting to go home, I felt
Eliza's secret something
whisper-shout, *You're a*
stranger here! I thought,
Yes. I thought, *I want*
my Mommy.

O My Mother
You've sent me
pricks of memory
of another house,
and another set of quilts,
and another family
with another Brother,
and another Father,
and you, another
Mother, a woman
with black hair.

Exile
She knows what it's
like to be cast out
into the wilderness
and the solitary place
and to make even
the desert rejoice,
and sing, and blossom
as the rose, anyway.

What Ashmae Taught Me
One time, in the temple,
after looking, and smelling,
and asking, and listening,
a quietness spoke back
that got louder and louder,
pressing words into
palms and the fleshy
tablet of the heart.
It said, *She* said:
Spread my name
like wildfire—
like wildflowers,
like wild forests.
So we did.

Too Sacred
The Mother is
too sacred
to *not* tallk about.

My Bones Whisper
She's real.
She's real.
She's real.

Home in the Wilderness
She is my home
in the wilderness
with all of the warm
and cozy things
I could wish for—a kettle,
my favorite tea, a fire,
music, a weighted blanket,
pumpkin banana bread
muffins, stacks of books—
but even without all
of those things
She is home.

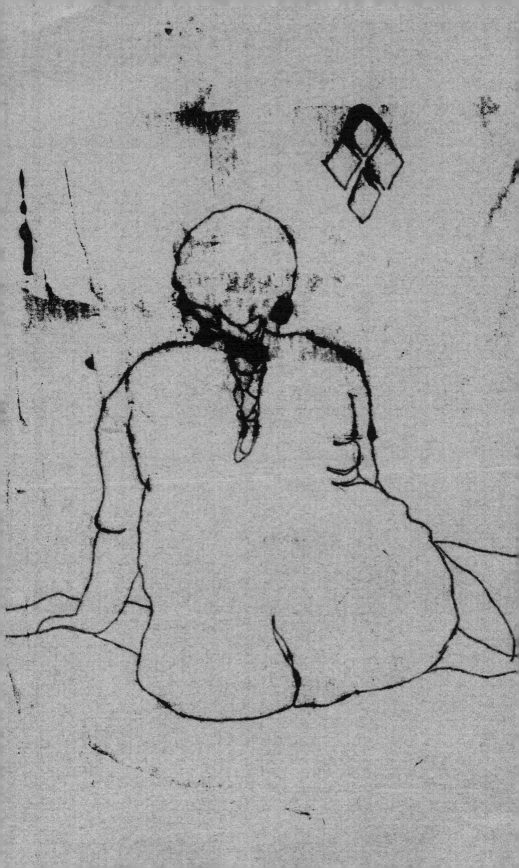

A Memory
My son (2)
on his knees,
arms folded
on his lap,
eyes open,
praying,
Mama,
Mama,
Mama.
Amen.

Something Close to a Prayer
Dear Mama,
do you know me?
Do you love me?
Are you still my
truest friend?
(I've made a lot
of mistakes.)

Love,
Rachel, your daughter

I Know Heavenly Mother Loves Me
I know Heavenly Mother loves me
when I pause, when I ask, when I listen,
when I see stars after years of not
seeing stars for a veil of light pollution
that is hard to break, when leaves change
in fall, and when I do.

I know Heavenly Mother loves me
when friends pause, and ask, and listen
sitting beside me in my grief
or joy, when crocuses and tulips
push their heads toward the air,
when I hear Søren learn a new word
or Cora sing a new song,
when words flow through me
of Her.

Heavenly Mother Knows We Love Her
Heavenly Mother
knows we love Her
when we do.

Proxy Mothers

I.

A woman I didn't know
well read my words
about the Mother sending
proxies, having authority
and shared with me
something she wanted
to share before, but
felt too nervous,
how when I was in
the hospital, she cared
for my children, which
I knew, after recently
moving to my city, which
I also knew, but that she
had more recently taken
a failed pregnancy test
and weaned her youngest
son, which I didn't know,

leaving her empty and
heavy at the same time.
Until she held my son,
who was six months
that day, and who I was
terrified would be hungry.
He had never drunk milk
that wasn't directly from
my breast, not even when
it was pumped into a bottle.
The woman offered him a bottle,
and he refused, choosing
to cry and cry instead.
Until. She offered him
her breast, becoming
a proxy Mother, and
he accepted.

II.
The day I was hospitalized,
my daughter asked my
husband for pancakes.
He said no. She asked again
and again. He said no
and no. He didn't know
I had made them for her that
morning and may have been
why she was asking, but a bit
later he saw a plate of pancakes
on our doorstep like cookies
or homemade bread, left by
another woman I didn't know
well, who had a feeling.
What I know, is that at three,
my daughter called out to
the universe and the Mother
answered and that both of
my children were fed.

Poem notes

At a Pulpit   First written for the "Handed Down and Altered" exhibit at the 2018 NYC Center for Latter-day Saint Arts Festival.

Poetry Mommy   Cora.

Girl Moon   Cora Steenblik and Larry Hunt.

What Joel Taught Me   Joel 2:28–29 "And it shall come to pass afterward, that I will pour out my spirit upon all flesh; and your sons and your daughters shall prophesy, your old men shall dream dreams, your young men shall see visions: And also upon the servants and upon the handmaids in those days will I pour out my spirit."

The Power   Naomi Alderman's *The Power*.

As an Eagle   Exodus 19:4 "Ye have seen what I did unto the Egyptians, and how I bare you on eagles' wings, and brought you unto myself."

As an Eagle, II   Deuteronomy 32:11–12 "As an eagle stirreth up her nest, fluttereth over her young, spreadeth abroad her wings, taketh them, beareth them on her wings: So the Lord alone did lead him, and there was no strange god with him."

As a Bear   Hosea 13:8 "I will meet them as a bear that is bereaved of her whelps, and will rend the caul of their heart, and there will I devour them like a lion: the wild beast shall tear them."

The Great She Is   *The Exponent II*, http://www.exponentii.org/.

What Sofia Taught Me   Via Sofia Jones.

Ampersand   Naomi Watkins and *Aspiring Mormon Women*, http://aspiringmormonwomen.org/.

What Lin Taught Me   Washington: "I'm not a maiden in need of defending, I am grown." Hamilton: "Charles Lee, Thomas Conway, these men take your name and they rake it through the mud." Washington: "My name's been through a lot, I can take it." Lin Manuel Miranda, "Meet Me Inside," *Hamilton*.

The Graver   Isaiah 49:16 "Behold, I have graven thee upon the palms of my hands; thy walls are continually before me."

What Anna Taught Me Anna Quindlen: "When someone asks you where you come from, the answer is your mother." *One True Thing*.

Your Mother Who is In Heaven Gives Good Gifts Matthew 7:9–11 "Or what man is there of you, whom if his son ask bread, will he give him a stone? Or if he ask a fish, will he give him a serpent? If ye then, being evil, know how to give good gifts unto your children, how much more shall your Father which is in heaven give good things to them that ask him?"

She Succors the Weak D&C 81:5 "Wherefore, be faithful; stand in the office which I have appointed unto you; succor the weak, lift up the hands which hang down, and strengthen the feeble knees."

What Chelsea Taught Me Chelsea Shields paired with Janice Kapp Perry's "A Child's Prayer."

What Wonder (Re)Taught Me "'On opening night, my parents were all the way in back of the auditorium, like where Jack is right now, but when the lights are off, you can't really see that far back. So I was like, 'Where are my parents? Where are my parents?' And then Mr. Resnick, our theater-arts teacher last year—he said: 'Charlotte, stop being such a diva!' And I was like, 'Okay!' And then I spotted my parents and I was totally fine. I didn't forget a single line.'" R.J. Palacio's *Wonder*, 27.

Sometimes "'My dear, I am the goddess of foresight and the immediate future. I would never tell you what to do. I am only here to give you the information you need to make a good choice. As to why you should listen to me, I hope you would do so because I love you.' 'LOVE ME?' Mallory looked at us in disbelief, like Are you hearing this? 'Old woman, I don't even know who you are!' 'Of course you do, dear.' The woman's form shimmered. Before us sat a middle-aged woman of regal beauty, her long hair the same color as Mallory's plaited down both shoulders. Her hat became a war helm of white metal, glowing and flickering like trapped neon gas. Her white dress seemed made of the same stuff, only woven into gentle folds. In her knitting bag, her fuzzy yarn had become swirling puffs of mist. The goddess, I realized, had been knitting with clouds. 'I am Frigg,' she said, 'queen of the Aesier. I am your mother, Mallory Keen.'" Rick Riordan's *The Ship of the Dead*. Via JaneAnne Peterson.

Mother Time Nancy Ross: "The figure itself recalls the iconography of the ancient Greek Hellenistic sculpture *Nike of Samothrace*, with its lack of head, wings, and drapery folds. In a Mormon context, I read this figure as a suggestion of Heavenly Mother as Mother Time, who is divine and yet embedded in the ordinary elements of Mormon women's lives. She is shut away in an attractive glass case, both present and distant, symbolically visible but unavailable." "Review: 50 Contemporary Women Artists: Groundbreaking Contemporary Art from 1960 to Now." *The Exponent Blog*. https://www.the-exponent.com/review-50-contemporary-women-artists-groundbreaking-contemporary-art-from-1960-to-now/. Michael: "This is Tuesdays. And also July." Janet: "And sometimes it's never." Michael: "That's true. Occasionally that moment on the Bearimie timeline is the time moment when nothing, ever occurs. So. You get it." *The Good Place*.

Tiptoes *The Good Place*, sort of.

A Mother Cries Inspired by Hannah Pritchett's, "What Duccio Taught Me": "Sometimes | a God weeps | And a Mother is tired. | She loves me, | And holds me, | But her eyes beg for a break."

What Margaret Taught Me Margaret Toscano: "She is with the dying, She is with the woman in labor, She cries with the outcast."

Hidden Mother Inspired by Matt Page's artwork, "Hidden Mothers."

Lost Girl The lost boys and Wendy Darling from J.M. Barrie's *Peter Pan*.

Matryoshka Dolls Laurel Thatcher Ulrich once commented to me that most family history charts are visually very patriarchal. I started to think about what a matriarchal family history chart would look like and landed on Russian nesting dolls. It fits so well. I owe Tracy McKay thanks for the clean phrasing.

Mother Lines Inspired by separate conversations with Laurel Thatcher Ulrich and Caitlin Connolly. Caitlin noted that in all of our mother lines, there's a point where the record breaks.

What Coco and Channing Taught Me Disney/Pixar's *Coco* paired with a lovely blog post by Channing Parker, http://www.channingbparker.com/2018/06/what-disneys-coco-taught-me-about.html.

What Heidi Taught Me Heidi Doxey: "It is passed unchanged from a mother to her children generation after generation. It doesn't mix with sperm so there's no rearrangement. You have the exact same mDNA as your mother, grandmother, and great-great-great-great-great-great grandmother. Your sons share your mDNA but they will not pass it to their children because it isn't in sperm, mDNA is passed exclusively along a maternal line and rarely mutates. There is perhaps one mutation every 10,000 years. In the entire world there are maybe 30ish strains of mDNA."

A Quilt Cut With Hands   Daniel 2:34–35 "Thou sawest till that a stone was cut out without hands, which smote the image upon his feet that were of iron or clay, and brake them to pieces. Then was the iron, the clay, the brass, the silver, and the gold, broken to pieces together, and became like the chaff of the summer threshingfloors; and the wind carried them away, that no place was found for them: and the stone that smote the image became a great mountain, and filled the whole earth."

After Creation   Inspired by Adam Miller's "Sabbath" chapter in the second edition of *Letters to a Young Mormon*. After creation, even God needed to rest. "Our Sabbath practice is meant to match God's own approach to his work of creation. In Genesis 1, God sets about creating the world. He works for six days. Then, 'on the seventh day God ended his work which he had made; and he rested on the seventh day" (Genesis 2:2). More, 'God blessed the seventh day, and sanctified it: because that in it he had rested from all his work which God created and made' (Genesis 2:3). This kind of rest is characteristic of God, and once he has blessed it, this kind of timeless rest becomes characteristic of the Sabbath itself. At the end of the sixth day, God "saw every thing that he had made, and, behold, it was very good' (Genesis 1:31)."

The Reason I Could Trust   Psalms 22:9 (KJV) "But thou art he that took me out of the womb: thou didst make me hope when I was upon my mother's breasts" paired with Psalms 22:9 New Living Translation (NLT) "Yet you brought me safely from my mother's womb and led me to trust you at my mother's breast."

Postpartum   "A very slight variation on *Mother's Milk*'s "Postpartum.""

Chrysalis   "And inside the chrysalis, it *changes*. Its body unmakes. Every portion of itself unravels, unwinds, undoes, and re-forms itself into something *else*. . . . The caterpillar goes into the chrysalis, her grandmother had said. And then it *changes*. Its skin changes and its eyes change and its mouth changes. Its feet vanish. Every bit of itself—even its knowledge of itself—turns to mush." Kelly Barnhill's *The Girl Who Drank the Moon*.

Quiet Place   The movie, *The Quiet Place*.

The Lamplighter   "When the little prince reached this planet, he greeted the lamplighter respectfully. 'Good morning. Why have you just put out your lamp?' 'Orders,' the lamplighter answered. 'Good morning.' 'What orders are those?' 'To put out my street lamp. Good evening.' And he lit his lamp again." *The Little Prince*, pop up book, 35.

C on the Holy Spirit   Cora.

Knocks   Revelation 3:20 "Behold, I stand at the door, and knock: if any man hear my voice, and open the door, I will come in to him, and will sup with him, and he with me."

Lost   Elizabeth Bishop's "One Art."

Something Soft as a Breast   Title from a line in Carol Lynn Pearson's poem, "Motherless House": "I live in a Motherless house. | I lie awake and listen always for the word that never comes, but might. | I bury my face | In something soft as a breast. | I am a child | Crying for my mother in the night.

Home   From Cora.

Where We Belong   Cora, again.

Somewhere to Lay His Head   Luke 9:58 "And Jesus said unto him, Foxes have holes, and birds of the air have nests; but the Son of man hath not where to lay his head."

What Spencer Taught Me   Spencer Steenblik.

Stretched   Jacob 5:47 "But what could I have done more in my vineyard? Have I slackened mine hand, that I have not nourished it? Nay, I have nourished it, and I have digged about it, and I have pruned it, and I have dunged it; and I have stretched forth mine hand almost all the day long … "

Her Brightness and Glory   Joseph Smith History 1:17 "… When the light rested upon me I saw two Personages, whose brightness and glory defy all description, standing above me in the air. One of them spake unto me, calling me by name and said, pointing to the other—This is My Beloved Son. Hear Him!"

Well Behaved Women   Laurel Thatcher Ulrich.

Like Emmeline   Emmeline B. Wells, "I believe in women, especially thinking women."

Relief   "Eliza R. Snow arose and said that … one objection to the word Relief is, that the idea associated with it is that of some great calamity—that we intend appropriating on some extraordinary occasions instead of meeting the common occurrences—Pres Emma Smith remark'd—we are going to do something extraordinary—when a boat is stuck on the rapids with a multitude of Mormons on board we shall consider that a loud call for relief—we expect extraordinary occasions and pressing calls—"

What Karim Taught Me   Karim Jones, on the border and empathy crises: "I would cross any border, I would climb any wall, I would do anything for [my children]."

Are You My Mother   P.D. Eastman's *Are You My Mother?*

French Parent   Pamela Druckerman's *Bringing Up Bébé.*

Through   Moses 5:10–11 "And in that day Adam blessed God and was filled, and began to prophesy concerning all the families of the earth, saying: Blessed be the name of God, for because of my transgression my eyes are opened, and in this life I shall have joy, and again in the flesh I shall see God. And Eve, his wife, heard all these things and was glad, saying: Were it not for our transgression we never should have had seed, and never should have known good and evil, and the joy of our redemption, and the eternal life which God giveth unto all the obedient."

What Fiona Taught Me   Fiona Givens.

The Pearl   Via Hugh Nibley's (and very partially Terryl Givens') retellings.

Psalm and **The Song**   In *Adam Miller's The Sun Has Burned My Skin.* "In the Bible, written for the most part from a male point of view, women are by definition the second sex. History is traced through the line of the fathers, as in priestly genealogies ('And Enoch begat Methuselah'), and the typical formulas for sexual relations ('he knew her,' 'he came into her,' 'he lay with her') make the woman seem passive and acted upon. But in the Song, where the lovers take turns inviting one another, desire is entirely reciprocal."

Lost and Found   Inspired in part by Brian Kershisnik's painting, "She Will Find What is Lost."

What Megan Taught Me and What Else Megan Taught Me   Megan Herles-Mooa.

Lost You   Elizabeth Whitesley.

They Arise   Malachi 4:2 "But unto you that fear my name shall the Sun of righteousness arise with healing in his wings; and ye shall go forth, and grow up as calves of the stall."

Of a Good Courage   Joshua 1:9 "Have not I commanded thee? Be strong and of a good courage; be not afraid, neither be thou dismayed: for the Lord thy God is with thee whithersoever thou goest."

What She Has Given   2 Timothy 1:7 "For God hath not given us the spirit of fear; but of power, and of love, and of a sound mind."

A Trail of Small Items   Title from Cora.

What Hannah Taught Me   Hannah Gadsby's *Nannette*.

All Day Long   2 Kings 6:15–17 "And when the servant of the man of God was risen early, and gone forth, behold, an host compassed the city both with horses and chariots. And his servant said unto him, Alas, my master! how shall we do? And he answered, Fear not: for they that be with us are more than they that be with them. And Elisha prayed, and said, Lord, I pray thee, open his eyes, that he may see. And the Lord opened the eyes of the young man; and he saw: and, behold, the mountain was full of horses and chariots of fire round about Elisha."

What Steve Taught Me   Steve Evans.

What Rilke Taught Me   "I only had streams of milk or tears to offer." Rainer Maria Rilke. "Before the Passion From the Life of Mary." Via Saskia Tielens.

A Prayer for Tomorrow, or The Other Side of Weaning   Inspired by Søren and also Carlee Dynes.

Listening For Answers   "We spoke mostly through cans and strings, is it any wonder we don't understand anything?" Book on Tapeworm, "Shadow Puppets." https://www.youtube.com/watch?v=iE_psUoBDgo.

Poet Laureate   Inspired by Tracy K. Smith.

What Steven Taught Me   "I paused and then screamed into the sky, 'Do you even know what love is? Does it even matter to you?'" … "'I know you think you are tainted. That you are poisoned. I tell you in no uncertain terms, you are not. You are a creature of love and nothing can touch that. Nothing.' 'But I am so broken.' 'Oh, my dear child, can't you see? We are all broken. It comes with existence.' Then she smiled, 'Broken yes, but not unhealed. Believe that.' I nodded, 'I do. I do believe it.' She turned to go, smiling once more at the rats, and as she did I said, 'Mother. Please take me with you.' She turned to me and smiled, her eyes moist and shining, 'Not yet. . . . But perhaps I can leave you with a blessing?' . . . 'I am weeping now just remembering the joy and feelings that poured from her mouth. . . . Until at last I was nursing, suckling at my mother's breast. Warm milk poured into my rooting mouth. No, it was not coming from my mother's breast, it was coming from the shepherdess's hands, pouring into me. . . . I cried and cried, but no tears of sorrow. The milk was healing me. Bringing me the life that mother's milk always brought. I was being brought back to life with every swallow.'" Steven Peck, *Gilda Trillim*.

What Joanna Taught Me   Joanna Brooks and *Mormon Feminism: Essential Writings*.

When She's Handed the Book   First written for the "Handed Down and Altered" exhibit at the 2018 NYC Center for Latter-day Saint Arts Festival, in response to Adam Miller's beautiful contribution, "Invocation."

She Carries the Book and **Big Home**   First written for the "Handed Down and Altered" exhibit at the 2018 NYC Center for Latter-day Saint Arts Festival.

What Cora Taught Me, or The Sun and Her Little Blooms   Borrowing heavily from Cora's poem "Little Blooms" for the "Handed Down and Altered" exhibit at the 2018 NYC Center for Latter-day Saint Arts Festival.

Her Name   Inspired by Cora.

What Cora Taught Me, One Million   C: "When I spin, I move the world." And: "I'm so dizzy, and the whole world is spinning."

What Rosie Taught Me   Rosemary Card.

What Maggie Taught Me   Via Maggie Smith (poet) and a t-shirt from The Bee & The Fox.

What Heather (Re)Taught Me   Heather Bergevin: ". . . thousands of tiny, unseen things."

What Sara Taught Me   Sara Vranes.

The Napping Place   Audrey and Don Woods' *The Napping House* paired with my Grandma Zena's constant invitation to nap.

The Mother Embodies Her Mother   Cora: "Comb it carefully."

The Mother Loves the World   For Shayla Frandsen.

Design Mom   Gabby Blair, *Design Mom* blog.

What Else Maggie Taught Me   "I'm desperate for you | to love the world because I brought you here." Maggie Smith's "First Fall."

What a Mother Does   Matthew 5:35–36 "For I was an hungred, and ye gave me meat: I was thirsty, and ye gave me drink: I was a stranger, and ye took me in: Naked, and ye clothed me: I was sick, and ye visited me: I was in prison, and ye came unto me."

What Zena Taught Me   Zena Hill.

The Knitter   Mosiah 18:21 "And he commanded them that there should be no contention one with another, but that they should look forward with one eye, having one faith and one baptism, having their hearts knit together in unity and in love one towards another." And: "I don't mind the weather, I've scarves, and caps, and sweaters. I've got long johns under slacks for blustery days." Death Cab For Cutie, "Blacking Out the Friction."

She Knows it By Heart   Merrijane Rice: "Record = re (again) + cord (heart). The heart used to be considered the seat of memory, as opposed to the brain. That's why we say we learn things 'by heart.'"

The Mother Cried Power   Hozier's "Nina cried power."

What Laurel Taught Me   Laurel Thatcher Ulrich.

What Rebecca Ann Taught Me   Rebecca Moore.

What Te Fiti Taught Me   *Moana*.

Climbing Mother   Inspired by Brian Kershisnik's painting of the same name, as well as his painting, "Mom Trick."

What the Exponent Taught Me   *Exponent II*, http://www.exponentii.org/.

How Heavens Weep   Moses 7:28 "And it came to pass that the God of heaven looked upon the residue of the people, and he wept; and Enoch bore record of it, saying: How is it that the heavens weep, and shed forth their tears as the rain upon the mountains?"

Why Heavens Weep   Moses 7: 33; 37 "And unto thy brethren have I said, and also given commandment, that they should love one another, and that they should choose me, their Father; but behold, they are without affection, and they hate their own blood … and the whole heavens shall weep over them, even all the workmanship of mine hands; wherefore should not the heavens weep, seeing these shall suffer?"

What Lisa Taught Me   Lisa Patterson Butterworth, "We Shall Find Kindness: Ordain Women and a Wound to the Body of Christ," https://www.feministmormonhousewives .org/2014/06/we-shall-find-kindness-ordain-women-and-a-wound-to-the-body-of -christ/.

What Joe and Gina Taught Me   Via an old poem by Joe Hunt and wise words from Gina Colvin.

Did Not Doubt   Alma 56:47–48: "Now they never had fought, yet they did not fear death; and they did think more upon the liberty of their fathers than they did upon their lives; yea, they had been taught by their mothers, that if they did not doubt, God would deliver them. And they rehearsed unto me the words of their mothers, saying: We do not doubt our mothers knew it.

Eleven   Netflix's *Stranger Things* S2.

Prodigal Daughter   Luke 15:17–20 "And when he came to himself, he said, How many hired servants of my father's have bread enough and to spare, and I perish with hunger! I will arise and go to my father, and will say unto him, Father, I have sinned against heaven, and before thee, And am no more worthy to be called thy son: make me as one of thy hired servants. And he arose, and came to his father. But when he was yet a great way off, his father saw him, and had compassion, and ran, and fell on his neck, and kissed him."

The Women at the Well   Inspired by Andrea Radke-Moss.

Blood Issues   Mark 5:26–34 "And a certain woman, which had an issue of blood twelve years, And had suffered many things of many physicians, and had spent all that she had, and was nothing bettered, but rather grew worse, When she had heard of

Jesus, came in the press behind, and touched his garment. For she said, If I may touch but his clothes, I shall be whole. And straightway the fountain of her blood was dried up; and she felt in her body that she was healed of that plague. And Jesus, immediately knowing in himself that virtue had gone out of him, turned him about in the press, and said, Who touched my clothes? And his disciples said unto him, Thou seest the multitude thronging thee, and sayest thou, Who touched me? And he looked round about to see her that had done this thing. But the woman fearing and trembling, knowing what was done in her, came and fell down before him, and told him all the truth. And he said unto her, Daughter, thy faith hath made thee whole; go in peace, and be whole of thy plague."

Our God   "God of our fathers, whose almighty hand | Leads forth in beauty all the starry band | Of shining worlds in splendor through the skies, | Our grateful songs before thy throne arise." Daniel C. Roberts. "God of our Father's, Whose Almighty Hand."

Jane   Jane Manning James, of course. "Jane's little group began walking the eight hundred miles to Nauvoo. Jane recalled: 'We walked until our shoes were worn out, and our feet became sore and cracked open and bled until you could see the whole print of our feet with blood on the ground. We stopped and united in prayer to the Lord, we asked God the Eternal Father to heal our feet and our prayers were answered and our feet were healed forthwith.' . . . 'The folks have all gone and got themselves homes, and I have got none.'" https://www.lds.org/ensign/1979/08/jane-manning-james-black-saint-1847-pioneer?lang=eng.

Emma   Emma Smith, of course.

Hewed Out   Proverbs 9: 1–3: "Wisdom hath builded her house, she hath hewn out her seven pillars: She hath killed her beasts; she hath mingled her wine; she hath furnished her table. She hath sent forth her maidens: she crieth upon the highest places of the city."

Maman and **What Louise Taught Me**   Amy Novesky, *Cloth Lullaby: The Woven Life of Louise Bourgeois*.

A House   "House that believes it is not a house," Tracy K. Smith's "Ash."

Grandmother   Tom Kimball.

What Terry Taught Me   Once in Northern California, Terry Tempest William's friend told her, "I heard the trees speaking. In my heart, I heard them say, 'We are struggling.'" "California's been in drought, I'm sure you're thirsty." "No, we're dying." Their roots were being crushed. "We are suffering." Terry said, "Give the grove back to the trees. Can we see this grove as a sacred place?" "The roots could breathe. Please listen. You are among elders. Can you hear them speaking?"

Like TTW   Terry Tempest Williams: "I pray to the birds. I pray to the birds because I believe they will carry the messages of my heart upward. I pray to them because I believe in their existence, the way their songs begin and end each day—the invocations and benedictions of Earth. I pray to the birds because they remind me of what I love rather than what I fear. And at the end of my prayers, they teach me how to listen." *Refuge: An Unnatural History of Family and Place.*

To Tree   "Tree speaks to stone; stone speaks to water. It is not so hard as we have supposed. Tell them to read what is written in the sky. Tell them to ask the rain! All of John Uskglass's old alliances are still in place. I am sending messengers to remind the stones and the sky and the rain of their ancient promises." Susanna Clarke, *Jonathan Strange and Mr. Norrell.*

What the Mother Prays To   Me: "What do you dream of?" C: "I dream of myself!" paired with Terry Tempest Williams: "I pray to the birds. I pray to the birds because I believe they will carry the messages of my heart upward. I pray to them because I believe in their existence, the way their songs begin and end each day—the invocations and benedictions of Earth. I pray to the birds because they remind me of what I love rather than what I fear. And at the end of my prayers, they teach me how to listen." *Refuge: An Unnatural History of Family and Place.*

Hub Tree   "The biggest, darkest nodes are the busiest nodes. We call those hub trees, or more fondly, mother trees, because it turns out that those hub trees nurture their young, the ones growing in the understory.... In a single forest, a mother tree can be connected to hundreds of other trees. And using our isotope tracers, we have found that mother trees will send their excess carbon through the mycorrhizal network to the understory seedlings, and we've associated this with increased seedling survival by four times. Now, we know we all favor our own children, and I wondered, could Douglas fir recognize its own kin, like mama grizzly and her cub? So we set about an experiment, and we grew mother trees with kin and stranger's seedlings. And it turns out they do recognize their kin. Mother trees colonize their kin with bigger mycorrhizal networks. They send them more carbon below ground. They even reduce their own root competition to make elbow room for their kids. When mother trees are injured or dying, they also send messages of wisdom on to the next generation of seedlings." Suzanne Simard's "How Trees talk to each other," TED Talk, https://www.ted.com/talks/suzanne_simard_how_trees_talk_to_each_other?language=en.

What Page Taught Me   Page Turner.

She Brave Woman   Inspired by a beautiful part of Ashley Mae Hoiland's beautiful book, *One Hundred Birds Taught Me to Fly: The Art of Seeking God*, that begins: "I MADE A BANNER that said "Be Brave" out of some old fabric I had dyed. I sewed it to a ribbon, and as I walked my kids to preschool one afternoon, we stopped at a set of trees that I knew many college students from the campus we lived on would pass by and tied the banner in place. For my whole life, no matter how hard I've tried, my work cannot escape from looking handmade, and so as the letters swung in the breeze, the banner looked anything but crisp and professional. I suspected that the banner would be taken down by campus security, vandalized, or blown down by wind and rain, but every so often my Remy, Thea, and I would take that path to school to check on our words in the trees, and there they remained, brave and immutable fabric vigilantes."

Hide-and-Seek III   Inspired by Claire Whitaker's "Hide and Seek."

She Casts the First and Last Stones   John 8:7 "So when they continued asking him, he lifted up himself, and said unto them, He that is without sin among you, let him first cast a stone at her"; Billie Hunt.

What Caitlin and Sarah Taught Me   Caitlin Connolly and Sarah Winegar.

The Artist   Inspired by Larry Hunt.

What Nate Taught Me   Nate Thatcher. All but the last line is his.

What Shaura Taught Me   Shaura Messervy.

I am Here   Isaiah 6:8 "Also I heard the voice of the Lord, saying, Whom shall I send, and who will go for us? Then said I, Here am I; send me."

Alpha and Omega   Inspired by Annie K. Blake on seeds, on one painted seed: "Is it the end or the beginning? Always both."

Where She Carries   "My heart is weak and unreliable. When I go it will be my heart. I try to burden it as little as possible. If something is going to have an impact, I direct it elsewhere. My gut for example, or my lungs, which might seize up for a moment but have never yet failed to take another breath. When I pass a mirror and catch a glimpse of myself … small daily humiliations—these I take, generally speaking, in the liver. Other damages I take in other places. The pancreas I reserve for being struck by all that's been lost. It's true that there's so much, and the organ is so small. But. You would be surprised how much it can take, all I feel is a quick sharp pain and then it's over. Sometimes I imagine my own autopsy. Disappointment in myself: right kidney. Disappointment of others in me: left kidney. . . . I don't mean to make it sound like I've made a science of it. It's not that well thought out. I take it where it comes. It's just that I notice certain patterns. When the clocks are turned back and the dark falls before I'm ready, this, for reasons I can't explain, I feel in my wrists. And when I wake up and my fingers are stiff, almost certainly I was dreaming of my childhood. The field where we used to play, the field in which everything was discovered and everything was possible. . . . Yesterday I saw a man kicking a dog and I felt it behind my eyes. I don't know what to call this, a place before tears. The pain of forgetting: spine. The pain of remembering: spine. All the times I have suddenly realized that my parents are dead, even now, it still surprises me, to exist in the world while that which made me has ceased to exist: my knees. . . . Loneliness: there is no organ that can take it all. Every morning, a little more." Nicole Krauss, *The History of Love.*

The Laughing God   Via Jason Kerr and Jacqueline Bussie.

What Paul Taught Me and **Other Things that Will Not Separate us From Her Love**   Romans 8:35; 37–39 "Who shall separate us from the love of Christ? Shall tribulation, or distress, or persecution, or famine, or nakedness, or peril, or sword? … Nay, in all these things we are more than conquerors through him that loved us. For I am persuaded, that neither death, nor life, nor angels, nor principalities, nor powers, nor things present, nor things to come, Nor height, nor depth, nor any other creature, shall be able to separate us from the love of God, which is in Christ Jesus our Lord"; Chieko Okazaki's rewriting: "For I am persuaded, that neither death, nor life, nor angels, nor principalities, nor powers, nor divorce, nor widowhood, nor children gone astray, nor infertility, nor little shortcomings, nor major mistakes nor poverty, nor lack of education, nor too much education, nor illness, nor sexual abuse, nor incest, nor singleness, nor insensitive leaders, nor gossip, nor spite, nor prejudice, nor feelings of guilt, nor feelings of inadequacy, nor loneliness, nor sorrow, nor pain nor any other creature, shall be able to separate us from the love of God, which is in Christ Jesus our Lord."

To Dress Her Body   First written for the "Handed Down and Altered" exhibit at the 2018 NYC Center for Latter-day Saint Arts Festival.

What Jason Taught Me   Jason Kerr.

What Else Jason Taught Me   Jason Kerr paired with D&C 89:20 "And shall run and not be weary, and shall walk and not faint."

Hyrum Dead/Jesus Dead   Title inspired by Jack Gilbert's "Machiko Dead."

The Most Moved Mover   Title inspired by Clark Pinnock's book of the same title.

What Rebecca Taught Me   Rebecca Davis Stevenson.

The Writing After the Disaster   Title inspired by Maurice Blanchot's *The Writing of the Disaster*.

The Mother Carries Tissue   Isaiah 25:8 "He will swallow up death in victory; and the Lord God will wipe away tears from off all faces; and the rebuke of his people shall he take away from off all the earth: for the Lord hath spoken it."

And Grace   D&C 84:98–99 "Until all shall know me, who remain, even from the least unto the greatest, and shall be filled with the knowledge of the Lord, and shall see eye to eye, and shall lift up their voice, and with the voice together sing this new song, saying: The Lord hath brought again Zion; The Lord hath redeemed his people, Israel, According to the election of grace, Which was brought to pass by the faith And covenant of their fathers."

What Else Page Taught Me   Page Turner.

Bloomsbury   Kyo Maclear and Isabelle Arsenault's *Virginia Wolf*.

My Daughter Teaches Me Where the Map Is   Cora.

What the Raven-haired Mother Taught Me   Kelly Barnhill's *The Girl Who Drank the Moon*.

Moonbeam   Nellie Talbot's "Jesus Wants Me for a Sunbeam."

Queen Bee   ". . . and then, her loss once known, after two or three hours, perhaps, for the city is vast, work will cease in almost every direction. The young will no longer be cared for; part of the inhabitants will wander in every direction, seeking their mother, in quest of whom others will sally forth from the hive; the workers engaged in constructing the comb will fall asunder and scatter, the foragers no longer will visit the flowers, the guard at the entrance will abandon their post; and foreign marauders, all the parasites of honey, forever on the watch for opportunities of plunder, will freely enter and leave without any one giving a thought to the defense of the treasure that has been so laboriously gathered. And poverty, little by little, will steal into the city; the population will dwindle; and the wretched inhabitants soon will perish of distress and despair, though every flower of summer burst into bloom before them." "The Swarm." Via Mikayla Thatcher.

Lament   Gina Colvin.

My Sorrow   Adam Daniel's *Blue Pop*.

Yokes   Matthew 11:29–30 "Take my yoke upon you, and learn of me; for I am meek and lowly in heart: and ye shall find rest unto your souls. For my yoke is easy, and my burden is light."

What Dar Taught Me   "You are the welcoming back from the ocean." Dar Williams' "The Ocean."

What Ariel Taught Me   A line from my nephew's elementary school play of *The Little Mermaid*.

Flora, Fauna, and Merryweather   Sleeping Beauty.

What Little Zina Taught Me   In which Andi Pitcher Davis' teenaged daughter, Zina, hand lettered "God is a woman. God is good. God is real. God loves you. God is a mother," and "~~Patriarchy~~," on a chalkboard in a Young Woman's room somewhere in Utah under a garland reading, "I am a child of God." The youth of Zion are not faltering.

Divine Nature   Melvin J. Ballard: "No matter to what heights God has attained or may attain, he does not stand alone; for side by side with him, in all her glory, a glory like unto his, stands a companion, the Mother of his children. For as we have a Father in heaven, so also we have a Mother there, a glorified, exalted, ennobled Mother." And: Vaughn J. Featherstone: "Women are endowed with special traits and attributes that come trailing down through eternity from a divine mother. Young women have special God-given feelings about charity, love, and obedience … theirs is a sacred, God-given role, and the traits they receive from heavenly mother are equally as important as those given to the young men."

Good Works   James 1:27 "Pure religion and undefiled before God and the Father is this, To visit the fatherless and widows in their affliction, and to keep himself unspotted from the world."

The Judge   That is, until She learned She can't judge without understanding. Maya Rudolph, *The Good Place*.

What Ruth Taught Me   Ruth Bader Ginsburg.

Moonstone   Title inspired by Maxine Hanks.

The Hour of Land   Terry Tempest Williams' *The Hour of Land*.

Peeling Back the Veil   Cora.

Unveiled   Mark 2:27–28 "And Jesus cried with a loud voice, and gave up the ghost. And the veil of the temple was rent in twain from the top to the bottom."

A Great Wonder   Revelation 12:1–2 "And there appeared a great wonder in heaven; a woman clothed with the sun, and the moon under her feet, and upon her head a crown of twelve stars: And she being with child cried, travailing in birth, and pained to be delivered."

Clothed   Proverbs 31:25 New Living Translation (NLT) "She is clothed with strength and dignity and laughs without fear of the future."

Crowns   Interpol's "NYC": "I had seven faces. I thought I knew which one to wear."

The Daughters of Miriam   Exodus 40:12–13 "And thou shalt bring Aaron and his sons unto the door of the tabernacle of the congregation, and wash them with water. And thou shalt put upon Aaron the holy garments, and anoint him, and sanctify him; that he may minister unto me in the priest's office"; Margaret Toscano: "And what about the priestly orders: Levitical, Aaronic, Patriarchal, Melchizedek, Enoch? Should they be used or should women be members of orders named after women of similar spiritual stature? If so, whose names should be used? Perhaps we can identify female equivalents for these orders. For example, Miriam, the sister of Moses and Aaron, may be an appropriate name to designate the women's lesser priesthood order: hence, the Miriamic priesthood." "Put on Your Strength O Daughters of Zion: Claiming Priesthood and Knowing the Mother," *Women and Authority*.

Zelophehad's Daughters   Numbers 27:1–7 "Then came the daughters of Zelophehad . . . Mahlah, Noah, and Hoglah, and Milcah, and Tirzah. And they stood before Moses, and before Eleazar the priest, and before the princes and all the congregation, by the door of the tabernacle of the congregation, saying, Our father died in the wilderness . . . and had no sons. Why should the name of our father be done away from among his family, because he hath no son? Give unto us therefore a possession among the brethren of our father. And Moses brought their cause before the Lord. And the Lord spake unto Moses, saying, The daughters of Zelophehad speak right: thou shalt surely give them a possession of an inheritance among their father's brethren; and thou shalt cause the inheritance of their father to pass unto them."

In My Mother's House   John 14:2–3 "In my Father's house are many mansions: if it were not so, I would have told you. I go to prepare a place for you. And if I go and prepare a place for you, I will come again, and receive you unto myself; that where I am, there ye may be also."

Wild Flock   Inspired, of course, by Mary Oliver's "Wild Geese."

Second Miracle   My own "First Miracles" paired with Edna St. Vincent Millay's "Figs From Thistles," "First Fig," and "Second Fig."

Names   Cora, of course.

Alma   "She had the most beautiful name he'd ever heard: Alma." "'The first woman may have been Eve, but the first girl will always be Alma. . . . If you remember the first time you saw Alma, you also remember the last. She was shaking her head. Or disappearing across a field. Or through your window. *Come back, Alma!* You shouted. *Come back! Come back!*'" "Alma. Who was she? My mother would say she was everyone, every girl and every woman that anyone ever loved." Nicole Krauss' *The History of Love*.

Billie   For Billie Hunt Patterson and Billie Evelyn Hunt.

Open-Handed   "'Will you make a hundred years of winter in a summer's day, or wake new snow-trees from the earth?' he said, and it was jeering. 'Will you raise your hand and mend the mountain's wounded face? When you have done these things, then truly will you be a Staryk queen.'" Naomi Novik's *Spinning Silver*.

The Name I Call Her   "My people will go into the flame with their names locked fast in their hearts; you will not have that of them, nor me . . . when I can no longer hold the mountain against his flames, at least my people will know that I have gone before them, and held their names in my heart until the end." Naomi Novik's *Spinning Silver*.

White Fruit   1 Nephi 8:10–12; 1 Nephi 11:8–9; 13–23 "And it came to pass that I beheld a tree, whose fruit was desirable to make one happy. And it came to pass that I did go forth and partake of the fruit thereof; and I beheld that it was most sweet, above all that I ever before tasted. Yea, and I beheld that the fruit thereof was white, to exceed all the whiteness that I had ever seen. And as I partook of the fruit thereof it filled my soul with exceedingly great joy.... And it came to pass that the Spirit said unto me: Look! And I looked and beheld a tree... and the beauty thereof was far beyond, yea, exceeding of all beauty; and the whiteness thereof did exceed the whiteness of the driven snow. And it came to pass after I had seen the tree... I beheld a virgin.... And it came to pass that I saw the heavens open; and an angel came down and stood before me; and he said unto me: Nephi, what beholdest thou? And I said unto him: A virgin, most beautiful and fair above all other virgins. And he said unto me: Knowest thou the condescension of God? And I said unto him: I know that he loveth his children; nevertheless, I do not know the meaning of all things. And he said unto me: Behold, the virgin whom thou seest is the mother of the Son of God, after the manner of the flesh. And it came to pass that I beheld that she was carried away in the Spirit; and after she had been carried away in the Spirit for the space of a time the angel spake unto me, saying: Look! And I looked and beheld the virgin again, bearing a child in her arms. And the angel said unto me: Behold the Lamb of God, yea, even the Son of the Eternal Father! Knowest thou the meaning of the tree which thy father saw? And I answered him, saying: Yea, it is the love of God, which sheddeth itself abroad in the hearts of the children of men; wherefore, it is the most desirable above all things. And he spake unto me, saying: Yea, and the most joyous to the soul."

Abish   Alma 19:16–17 "And it came to pass that they did call on the name of the Lord, in their might, even until they had all fallen to the earth, save it were one of the Lamanitish women, whose name was Abish, she having been converted unto the Lord for many years, on account of a remarkable vision of her father—Thus, having been converted to the Lord, and never having made it known, therefore, when she saw that all the servants of Lamoni had fallen to the earth, and also her mistress, the queen, and the king, and Ammon lay prostrate upon the earth, she knew that it was the power of God; and supposing that this opportunity, by making known unto the people what had happened among them, that by beholding this scene it would cause them to believe in the power of God, therefore she ran forth from house to house, making it known unto the people."

What Sara Katherine Taught Me   Sara Katherine Staheli Hanks, "Heavenly Mother and the Baader Meinhoff Phenomenon," https://www.feministmormonhousewives .org/2014/05/heavenly-mother-and-the-baader-meinhoff-phenomenon/.

The Mormon Women Project   *The Mormon Women Project,* https://www.mormonwomen.com/.

Mother in Heaven is for the ERA   Sara Evans: "By January 1979, Mormons for the ERA had grown to 500 members and they became a regular fixture at both Mormon gatherings–where airplanes drew 'Mormons for the ERA Are Everywhere' and 'Mother in Heaven Loves Mormons for the ERA' banners across the sky–and at pro-ERA events." *Tidal Wave: How Women Changed America at Century's End.* Found with the help of Miriam Murdock Higginbotham.

What's Her Name   Olivia Meikle and Katie Nelson, *What's Her Name Podcast,* https://www.whatshernamepodcast.com/.

Segullah   "In Hebrew segullah signifies a cherished personal possession that is set apart and diligently cared for; it is a term the Lord has used with affection to describe His covenant people (Exodus 19:5, Psalms 135:4), and one we use here in remembrance of the blessings and responsibilities we receive in relationship with Him." *Segullah* literary magazine, https://segullah.org/about/.

Sister's Quorum   *Sister's Quorum* blog, https://sistersquorum.com/.

Women's Work   D&C 25 3; 7–8; 11: "Behold, thy sins are forgiven thee, and thou art an elect lady, whom I have called. . . . And thou shalt be ordained under his hand to expound scriptures, and to exhort the church, according as it shall be given thee by my Spirit. For he shall lay his hands upon thee, and thou shalt receive the Holy Ghost, and thy time shall be given to writing, and to learning much. . . . And it shall be given thee, also, to make a selection of sacred hymns, as it shall be given thee, which is pleasing unto me, to be had in my church" and an aside from Claudia Bushman, that the work of women is not to clean and take care of children but to learn and to write.

What Rachel Taught Me   Rachel Farmer's exhibit, "Looking Forward, Looking Back," https://www.granaryarts.org/rachel-farmer-looking-forward-looking-back.

Nesting   Netflix's *Russian Doll*.

What Henri Taught Me   Henri Amiel: "The mother should consider herself as her child's sun, a changeless and ever radiant world, whither the small restless creature, quick at tears and laughter, light, fickle, passionate, full of storms, may come for fresh stores of light, warmth, and electricity, of calm and of courage. The mother represents goodness, providence, law; that is to say, the divinity, under that form of it which is accessible to childhood…. The religion of a child depends on what its mother and its father are; and not on what they say. The inner and unconscious ideal which guides their life is precisely what touches the child; their words, their remonstrances, their punishments, their bursts of feeling even, are for him [her] merely thunder and comedy; what they worship, this it is which his instinct divines and reflects. The child sees what we are, behind what we wish to be." Via Gary Gillum.

When Winter Still Sits in the Chair   Title inspired by Neil Gaiman's "October in the Chair."

What Amanda Taught Me   Amanda Farr.

The Work I've Made   Moses 1:4 "And, behold, thou art my son; wherefore look, and I will show thee the workmanship of mine hands; but not all, for my works are without end, and also my words, for they never cease."

YMF   Hannah Wheelwright, Kaitlin Adams, and Young Mormon Feminists; Matthew 5:45 "That ye may be the children of your Father which is in heaven: for he maketh his sun to rise on the evil and on the good, and sendeth rain on the just and on the unjust"; 2 Nephi 26:33 "… he inviteth them all to come unto him and partake of his goodness; and he denieth none that come unto him, black and white, bond and free, male and female; and he remembereth the heathen; and all are alike unto God, both Jew and Gentile."

Queen Noor   Q. Noor and Rosie Card.

Living With Her   Inspired by Li-Young Lee's poem of the same name.

What Miranda and Calvin Taught Me   Miranda July and Calvin Burke.

What Kerry Taught Me   Kerry Spencer.

Chosen Names   With help from Kimberly Anderson.

Hold On to These Names   Fiona Givens.

Sound Wisdom   Proverbs 8:14 "Counsel is mine, and sound wisdom: I am understanding; I have strength."

Asherah   Fiona Givens: "At a Symposium held in honor of Joseph Smith at the Library of Congress in 2004, the eminent scholar of temple theology, Margaret Barker, discusses the centrality of Christ and of His Priesthood to Solomon's—'the priests of the Most High after the order of Melchizedek, which was after the order of Enoch, which was after the Only Begotten Son.' She also describes the central—and long-since obscured—role of Wisdom in that Temple. Wisdom's symbol was the Menorah—a stylized, golden almond tree with a candlestick in the center and three branches on either side. Wisdom—the Feminine Divine, or The Mother in Heaven—has several names, perhaps the most prevalent of which are Asherah and El Shaddai (God with breasts) and her dominant symbol is a tree—specifically the Tree of Life. During the reign of King Josiah there arose a contestation between the Temple Priesthood and a group called the Deuteronomists with whom Josiah sided… In addition, 'hostility to Wisdom was a hallmark of the Deuteronomists, and due to their influence, the Mother and her tree have been almost forgotten—but not in the Book of Mormon.'" "Before the World Was, She Was," https://www.mormonwomen.com/sunday-school-supplements/lesson-seventeen/

David Dying   Bless David Paulsen forever. He changed everything; Dylan Thomas' "Do Not Go Gentle Into That Good Night."

What Martin Taught Me   Martin Pulido, who with David Paulsen, also changed everything.

What Deidre Taught Me   Deidre Green; Carol Lynn Pearson, "Millie's Mother's Red Dress."

Homesick   Eliza R. Snow's "O My Father."

O My Mother   O My Mother: "But the house and the quilts and the woman with the black hair—Luna had seen them before. But she didn't know where… There was another house. And another family. Before this house. And this family. She knew it in her bones." Kelly Barnhill's *The Girl Who Drank the Moon*. Title inspired by Eliza R. Snow's "O My Father."

Exile   Isaiah 35:1–2 "The wilderness and the solitary place shall be glad for them; and the desert shall rejoice, and blossom as the rose. It shall blossom abundantly, and rejoice even with joy and singing. . . . And the ransomed of the Lord shall return, and come to Zion with songs and everlasting joy upon their heads: they shall obtain joy and gladness, and sorrow and sighing shall flee away."

What Ashmae Taught Me   Ashley Mae Hoiland, *One Hundred Birds Taught Me to Fly: The Art of Seeking God.* "IN THE TEMPLE I put all my senses to work searching for Her. A painting on the wall depicting a woman holding a giggling child in the air above her. The chandelier in the celestial room with the flowers on the table below it. The scent of fresh laundry on my rented temple clothes, and I thought of all the women's hands gathering, washing, folding and distributing. I got tired and rested my chin on my chest while I sat quietly and felt that someone understood. I listened, and listened, and listened through the words that were spoken, through the racing thoughts of my own mind, through my questions; I listened and the quietness spoke back, a quietness that got louder and louder, until as I walked down the stairs back to the dressing room, the words pressed themselves into the palms of my hands and soft places of my heart—'Spread my name like wildfire.'"

Home in the Wilderness   Netflix's *Hilda*, S1:E11 Chapter 11 "The House in the Woods."

Something Close to a Prayer   Sufjan Stevens.

I Know Heavenly Mother Loves Me   Clara W. McMaster's "My Heavenly Father Loves Me"; Editors, "Push Your Head Towards the Air."

Art notes

Photo credit: Keri Michelle Photography

Rachel Hunt Steenblik is the award-winning author of *Mother's Milk: Poems in Search of Heavenly Mother*. She also researched Heavenly Mother full-time for the *BYU Studies* article, "'A Mother There': A Survey of Historical Teachings about Mother in Heaven" and co-edited *Mormon Feminism: Essential Writings* for Oxford University Press. She finished her PhD coursework in philosophy of religion and theology at Claremont Graduate University and has a BA in philosophy from Brigham Young University and an MS in library and information science from Simmons College. She currently lives in Wenzhou, China with her family where she mothers, writes, and teaches the occasional class.

huntsteenblik.com   @rachelsteenblik

Ashley Mae Hoilandis the author and illustrator of the award-winning book, *One Hundred Birds Taught Me to Fly*. Her writing has appeared in many publications, both online and in print. She is the illustrator of *Mother's Milk* by Rachel Hunt Steenblik. She has written and illustrated six children's books and is the founder of the We Brave Women project. She received a BFA in painting and an MFA in creative writing from Brigham Young University. She is the co-founder of Mine To Tell, a space that teaches women to find their own strength through creative writing. More can be found on her website, Ashmae.com and at Minetotell.com. She currently lives in Santa Cruz, California with her husband and three children.

ashmae.com

Made in the USA
Monee, IL
27 September 2020